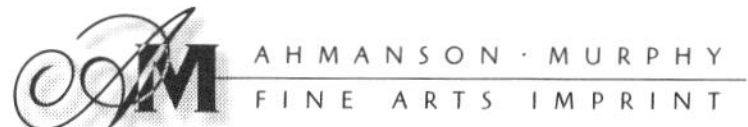

THE AHMANSON FOUNDATION

has endowed this imprint

to honor the memory of

FRANKLIN D. MURPHY

who for half a century

served arts and letters,

beauty and learning, in

equal measure by shaping

with a brilliant devotion

those institutions upon

which they rely.

*The publisher gratefully acknowledges the generous
support of the Art Endowment Fund of the University
of California Press Foundation, which was established
by a major gift from the Ahmanson Foundation.*

*The publisher also gratefully acknowledges
the generous contribution to this book
provided by George Mason University.*

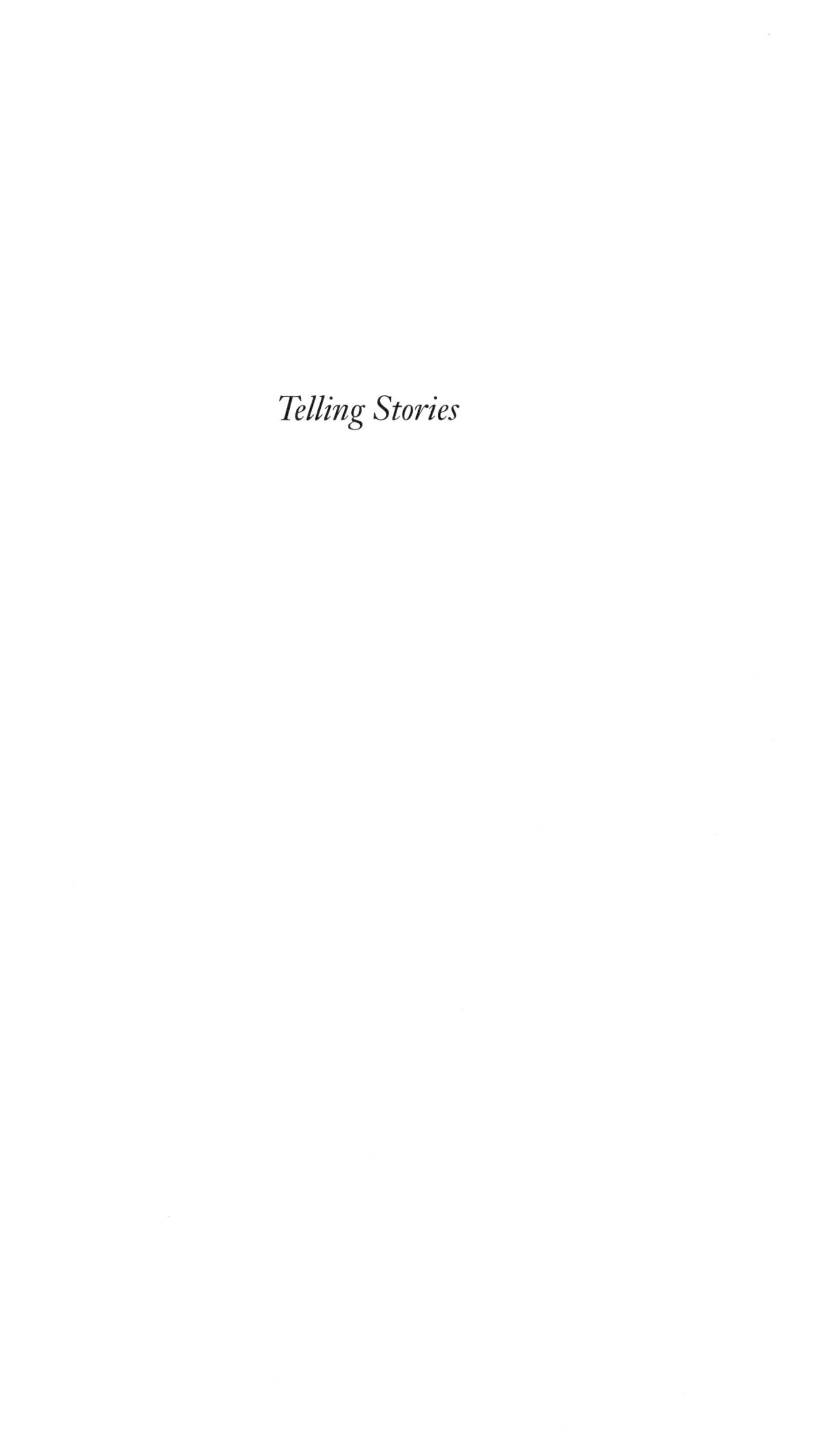

Telling Stories

Telling Stories

Philip Guston's Later Works

David Kaufmann

UNIVERSITY OF CALIFORNIA PRESS

Berkeley   Los Angeles   London

University of California Press, one of the most distinguished
university presses in the United States, enriches lives around
the world by advancing scholarship in the humanities, social
sciences, and natural sciences. Its activities are supported by
the UC Press Foundation and by philanthropic contributions
from individuals and institutions. For more information,
visit www.ucpress.edu.

University of California Press
Berkeley and Los Angeles, California

University of California Press, Ltd.
London, England

© 2010 by The Regents of the University of California

Library of Congress Cataloging-in-Publication Data

Kaufmann, David
   Telling stories : Philip Guston's later works / David
Kaufmann.
      p. cm.
   Includes bibliographical references and index.
   ISBN 978-0-520-26575-2 (cloth : alk. paper)—
   ISBN 978-0-520-26576-9 (pbk. : alk. paper)
   1. Guston, Philip, 1913–1980—Criticism and
interpretation.   I. Guston, Philip, 1913–1980.
II. Title.   III. Title: Philip Guston's later works.
ND237.G8K35   2010
759.13—dc22   2010002016

Manufactured in the United States of America

19   18   17   16   15   14   13   12   11   10
10   9   8   7   6   5   4   3   2   1

The paper used in this publication meets the minimum
requirements of ANSI/NISO Z39.48-1992 (R 1997)
(*Permanence of Paper*).

For Sharon, Zoe, and Lucia

The magic of compound
Interest the agency of the smallest
Degree.

CONTENTS

Plates follow page 54

Introduction

1

1. Sick of Purity

6

2. Thinking Thoughtlessness

28

3. Allegory

53

4. Jewish Jokes

71

Acknowledgments

91

Notes

93

Index

113

INTRODUCTION

The title of this book derives from Philip Guston's somewhat testy explanation of his return to figuration after years of abstract painting, a return highlighted by an exhibition at the Marlborough Gallery in New York in the fall of 1970: "I got sick and tired of all that Purity! wanted to tell Stories!"[1] While Guston was a prominent Abstract Expressionist, he had never been strongly allied to Clement Greenbergian modernism. He drew heavily on Giorgio de Chirico, both early and late, and he took as his models Max Beckmann and the Pablo Picasso of the twenties. Guston's pantheon of renegades from modernism included James Ensor, as Guston explained in a 1977 letter to Harold Rosenberg:

> The strongest "Pull" of Ensor on me (particularly the late work) was his courage, independence finally from the myths of "Modern Art." To dare to use narrative, the "mysterious" story being told which holds us so strongly. . . . The rest—that "modern art" which *accepts* its own limitations—of its means— becomes elegant and conventional—it . . . loses the *new.*[2]

Guston's rejection of the "myths of 'Modern Art'" and his embrace of stories at a time when *literary* was a term of abuse were clearly meant to be provocative and not a little perverse.

In their form and content the stories that Guston painted ran counter to the stories that art historians and critics of the late sixties were used to telling. Not surprisingly, the "new Gustons" of 1970 received a famously chilly reception. Nevertheless, Guston returned to favor in the mid-seventies and, by the time of his death in 1980, was considered—by some, at least—the exemplary painter of his time. And then the story took another twist. Between 1980 and 2000 only one monograph about him got published. Although his work appeared in a number of shows, there was only one major retrospective of his work. In the past decade, his stock has risen once again.

In the chapters that follow, I look at all these stories. I argue that Guston's willfully clumsy, gutsy, and often beautiful "cartoons" were a direct reaction to the rapid obsolescence of style that the art market of the 1960s demanded. Some critics attacked them because they did not fit into the reigning narratives of the day. But Guston did more than turn his back on the vanguard practices of the time. By incorporating without condescension and without irony American high modernism's rejected others—the philistine, the banal, and the vulgar—Guston's paintings refused the glamour and the authority of the avant-garde on which both modernism and postmodernism rested.

Philip Guston (born Phillip Goldstein) came to see the lure of the avant-garde and of modernist principles as the mask of a universalism that could never quite be universal. His later paintings solicited the "philistine" audience, played slapstick games with the banal as well as with evil, and courted a sticky-pink and sometimes sentimental vulgarity. If they were not an affirmation of his immigrant, working-class Jewish background, they were at least an acknowledgment of it. In this regard Guston's case makes an interesting comparison with those of Mark Rothko (who tried to turn his Judaism into an unaffiliated religiosity) and Barnett Newman (who tried to recast Judaism's theological commitments into a potent series of metaphors). Guston's later work does not directly engage the religious content of Judaism. Rather, it derives from the artist's position as a Jew. In the end, of course, the paintings cannot be subsumed by Guston's ambivalence about his identity. But we misunderstand Guston's particularity—his project and his achievement—if we try to ignore it.

Some words about method and terminology. In this book I discuss a number of art critics because it seems clear—even banal—that artworks become meaningful in relation to the art world of their time. But Guston presents an interesting case, because adverse criticism often got his paintings right, though for the wrong reasons, and these critics therefore usually came to the wrong conclusions.

Let me be more precise about what I understand by the term *art world*. It represents a self-enclosed and therefore relatively independent sphere of activity with its own criteria for excellence and its own entrance and exit procedures. When Arthur Danto argued in 1964 that works of art required an art world, a network that could establish the distinction between artworks and "real things," he was more interested in his own theory of what he called "indiscernibles" than in the concrete organization of the art world.[3] As befits a philosopher, Danto needed only to nod to sociology. For his purpose the institutions of the art world did not need to be described any more specifically than "a loose affiliation of individuals who know enough by way of theory and history that they are able to practice . . . historical explanations of works of art."[4] Danto provided no explanation of where and how these people might find each other, the means by which they might seal their affiliation, or how they might pay the rent. Danto's art world consists of disembodied individuals looking at embodied meanings (his description of works of art) in undefined spaces. But the counterintuitive bloodlessness of Danto's "discourse of reasons" does present us with still another problem. His account smoothes over the important and heated aesthetic debates that marked the 1960s. Reading Danto's famous account, you would not know that Andy Warhol's *Brillo Boxes*—the works that served as the immediate occasion of Danto's essay on the art world—were not greeted with universal and enduring acclaim.

At the other extreme Pierre Bourdieu's elegant sociological maps of the field of cultural production are about nothing so much as these conflicts between reasons.[5] Bourdieu's art world consists of embodied people in real spaces, but he reduces the antagonists' aesthetic positions directly to their social position in relation to symbolic and financial capital. While he shows how strategic moves within the art world are geared toward improving one's social and financial situation, he is apt to fall into an essentialism based on class.[6] Accordingly, he is not particularly interested in the rationality of the reasons given for those moves. In other words, while Danto sees the history and the theory of art as the logical unfolding of certain problems, Bourdieu is apt to present the theoretical debates that animate the art world as mere rationalizations in a war of position. In fact, as the *Brillo Boxes* (and Danto's famous reaction) show, positions in the art world can be created by following the rational paths that different lines of aesthetic reasoning open up.

The argument of the chapters that follow takes seriously both the discourse of reasons that provides the intellectual and ideological integration of the art world and the conflicts and competitions that provide its dynamism. It may also appear "idealist" and unduly fascinated with the self-descriptions of artists, critics, and curators. While I do pay too little attention to the art market's everyday forms of getting and spending, I would be more bothered by this omission if I did not have in mind Bourdieu's account of the apparent inversion of economic laws on which the field of cultural production depends. High culture—especially visual art—tends to disavow its interest in immediate profits because it is geared toward long-term returns. Its alchemy transforms reputation and scandal into negotiable assets, although only over the long haul.[7] Of course, it is true that since the 1960s the time required for conversion of symbolic capital into cash money has shortened considerably, but a necessary lag still exists between succès d'estime and real wealth. As they were in 1950 and in 1970, recognition and reputation remain the coin of the realm of art for us. To worry about reasons and recognition—as the chapters that follow will do—is ultimately to worry about money in however mediated a way.

Sick of Purity

In October and November 1970 you could have traced a respectable history of the American avant-garde by going from museum to gallery to museum in New York. Had you wanted, you could have progressed from the glory days of the Alfred Stieglitz circle to Abstract Expressionism and on to Pop. You could have then proceeded to Minimalism and Postminimalism and ended with the most contemporary of movements, site-specific Earthworks. Your tour would have taken you from Georgia O'Keeffe (at the Whitney) to Jane Freilicher and Red Grooms (at Myers), Robert Mangold and Alex Katz (at Fischbach), Roy Lichtenstein and James Rosenquist (at Castelli), Lucas Samaras (at Pace), Larry Poons (at Rubin), Brice Marden (at Bykert), Carl Andre (at the Guggenheim), and, finally, Richard Long (at Dwan). It is not too much to say that the previous fifty years of art all were on view somewhere in the city that fall.

According to Charlotte Lichtblau's survey of the exhibitions then on view in New York, the sheer availability of modernism gave contemporary artists enormous license. Artists could begin anywhere. Every revolutionary break with the past, she said, had been shown to be "yet another link in the chain of tradition." As the logic of artistic schools and movements had played itself out, it was "up to the individual artist to find his own place."[1] Everything, it seems, was up for grabs.

Against this background we can begin to understand what Philip Guston was up to when he returned to New York that fall to mount an exhibition at the Marlborough Gallery. The show, which featured figurative paintings completely unlike the earlier abstractions that had made him a respected member of the New York School, was his first in four years. The works featured the blocky shapes and open brushwork that had marked Guston's abstract paintings of the early 1960s. Now, however, the blocks had become people and things. They turned into boxy cars, Krazy Kat mesas, and, most important, human figures that Guston called "Hoods" (plate 1).

The size of the works lent them both Abstract Expressionism's sublime heroism and some of the mock heroics of Pop art. The heavy black outlines reminded a number of critics of cartoons.[2] And, of course, they do evoke the comics. But the comic strips to which they refer, whether *Krazy Kat, L'il Abner,* or *Mutt and Jeff,* differ from the straight-edge comic books of the 1940s and 1950s favored by Roy Lichtenstein. Guston's figures are the very antithesis of slick industrial draftsmanship and mass reproduction. Their clunkiness stands as a blunt reminder of their status as free-hand drawings.

At first glance *City Limits* (1969; plate 1) has little to do with Guston's shimmery abstractions of the 1950s. But as Frank O'Hara noted in 1962, Guston had taken an idiosyncratic path to Abstract

Expression. According to O'Hara, Guston had been led by the cockeyed landscapes of Surrealism and not the flatness of Cubism. Hence his abstract paintings, with their "hierarchical attitude toward form," preserved the distinction between foreground and background that belonged to the history of figuration.[3] He had always been influenced by Max Ernst and the Pablo Picasso of the 1920s, and his later works owed much to Giorgio de Chirico and Max Beckmann.[4] Guston's works imagined another history of modernism—not the one that prevailed in New York in the 1950s and 1960s.

O'Hara wrote that particular impulses and interests had brought Guston to abstraction after World War II. Similarly particular impulses and interests brought him back to figuration at the end of the 1960s. A decade earlier Guston had rejected the abstractionist credo that contemporary art was self-contained and therefore self-referential. In an irritated response to Ad Reinhardt at the "Philadelphia Panel" in 1960, Guston said that there was "something ridiculous and miserly" in the myth that painting was "pure and for itself." Art, according to Guston, was by definition impure and its history was determined by "adjustment of 'impurities.'"[5] Guston was attacking Reinhardt's fierce defense of the notion that art is about its medium, that it guards its boundaries by ignoring what lies outside. While Guston seemed to agree with Clement Greenberg that the history of art was continuous and not a series of absolute breaks, Guston rejected the idea that this history consisted of the progressive elimination of conventions (illusion, perspective, and the like), as Greenberg had argued. Rather, Guston said that adjusting the conventions was the very stuff of art history.

Guston discussed his understanding of "painting's continuities" in his 1965 article "Faith, Hope and Impossibility." He maintained they were the product of learning over and over again that creation is merely momentary. While it serves as "both the lie and the mask of art," it also mortifies art. Artistic creation maintains art's illusions and serves to critique those illusions. This difficult double play makes up the continuity of art.[6] Aesthetic traditions are never definitively discarded. In order for there to be any art at all, conventions must be continuously undone and rethought. Art's history is really a narrative of the way that single works engage and negate conventions. Single works and not schools or movements. Grand narratives about art did not interest Guston. He wanted to concentrate on the way that every painting justified itself. He felt that there were enough paintings in the world. Every painting had to justify itself, had to "eliminate the air of the arbitrary as completely as possible."[7] Every painting had to prove that its necessity lay in its relation to truth and to the objects of this world.

Guston expressed this view most clearly in a dense, counterintuitive article from the spring of 1965 in which he read the enigmas of Piero della Francesca's Arezzo cycle as the expression of anxiety about where things "can be located," and, more important, he asked, "in what condition can everything exist?" Guston suggested that painting's legitimacy rests on its ability to find where and how things *should* be located in pictorial space. But an individual painting may fall short and present an image—the spatial interrelation of object and people—that ultimately fails to show where everything *really* belongs. And that is where the problem lies. The painter risks freezing things while they are still on the move, that is, before the image reaches its proper disposition. *The Baptism of Christ* displays the double bind that confronts every painter who tries to get it right and therefore risks getting it permanently wrong. Guston claimed that Piero's painting is not marked by its apparent hieratic calm. It is, instead, "a vast precaution to avoid immobility, a wisdom that can include the partial doubt about the final destiny of forms."[8]

Five months after the Piero essay, Guston claimed that the painter is confronted with the problem of "fixing" a tolerable image. *Fixing* is an ambiguous word. It can mean securing something or repairing it. For Guston, though, the two meanings blended into one, for nailing a thing to its correct place is to repair it. So the artist must decide "what can be where," he said. Personal desire cannot enter the decision because the final state of the world has nothing to do with the painter's emotions or desires. A painting depicts a necessary reality. Desire, on the other hand, is incomplete and arbitrary.[9]

Art, then, was about the process of discovering a truthful image through the act of painting. The painter does not know beforehand what the image will actually look like in the end. This cloud of unknowing is the condition of modern painting. Guston maintained that during the Renaissance the artist and audience shared a "foreknowledge of what was going to be brought into existence." Drawing on Richard Wollheim's article "Minimal Art," which had appeared a short time earlier, Guston called that foreknowledge "pre-imaging." He argued that we can no longer "act as if pre-imaging is possible."[10] The common rules and conventions that made up the "pre-image" had disappeared.

In the Piero essay the problem of the image was the transhistorical problem of painting. Barely half a year later Guston had changed his diagnosis. The anxiety surrounding the image was historical and described the peculiar fate of modernism. The artist no longer had the benefit of a shared sense of where objects should actually be. No longer could the painter imagine a point from which perspective could capture the final destiny of things. Hence the contemporary painter not only confronted the continual danger of error but was also the victim of the depletion of certainty. Guston had already spoken of this depletion in the late 1950s: "I do not see why the loss of faith in the known image and symbol in our time should be celebrated as a freedom. It is a loss from which we suffer."[11] Abstraction was not the formal emancipation of painting from contingent conventions. Rather, it acknowledged the historical impoverishment of art.

New Place (1964; plate 2) is a good example of what Guston meant when he wrote that the task of painting is to locate things in their proper places. Like most of Guston's paintings of this period, it takes the stages of its own composition as its subject. The margins of the canvas are unpainted, and the broad thick application allows the pink underpainting to show through. White paint cancels black brushstrokes, leaving ghostly traces of gray along an equally ghostly vertical and horizontal lattice. (Guston referred to his technique as "erasure.")[12] Diagonals and the occasional curve disrupt right angles. Shadows of black shapes lower, especially to the viewer's right in the bottom third of the painting. Three unequal masses—one that is roughly square and two that are more oblong—have broken through the gray. To be more accurate, they *remain*. They lurk toward the middle of the canvas. Their interrelation is tense, as is their ambiguous emergence from their background.

At this stage of his career Guston's paintings tended to build from the edges. This allowed him to signal the way that the revisions had produced the painting's image over time. Despite their insistent mass, the apparitions in his works are ambiguously uneven because their exact contours are always unclear. In this way their relationship to each other is also tenuous, because it is time bound and contingent. The image is nothing less than the drama and uncertainty of its coming into focus. It displays Guston's effort to avoid immobility.

Guston published "Faith, Hope and Impossibility" in 1965, the year after he painted *New Place*. Together they displayed an existential, even moral, urgency. Nevertheless, after Guston showed at the Jewish Museum in 1966, he was unable to paint for another two years. Between 1965 and 1966 the imperatives that had driven Guston's abstract work disappeared.

Even if Guston had not been the most financially successful member of the New York School, he had always been well respected. He had exhibited regularly and had won prestigious awards. He had been granted the very first one-man show at the Guggenheim Museum in 1962. But the world had changed. Critics generally ignored Guston's 1966 exhibition at the Jewish Museum. Barry Schwabsky has speculated that the lack of critical attention made Guston realize that he had "somehow been exiled to the margins of a historical process of which [he] had once been at the center."[13] And indeed the defensiveness of Sam Hunter's catalogue essay for the Jewish Museum betrayed a real fear that Guston's work, because it was abstract and painterly, was no longer relevant. "The obsession of fashion with novelty," Hunter wrote, "makes us impatient with known personalities and styles, often on grounds of familiarity alone."[14] Guston was familiar, and Abstract Expressionism, which had justified itself in terms of its novelty and its definitive breaks with the past, had receded into that past. Hunter appealed to the "finer nuance" of Guston's work, but even that smacked of an old-fashioned connoisseurship.

At fifty-three Guston had become a stolid representative of "older art." But Hunter also indicated that Guston had painted himself into a corner. Guston had become fixated on a "limited ensemble of forms" and exhibited a "restricted range of expressive handling." Because the painter was "dominated by a single idea," he "flirted with monotony." His works "provide . . . little relief in the way of possible change." While Hunter tried to argue that Guston's apparent weaknesses derived from a singleness of vision, the critic was reflecting the reality of Guston's situation. The art audience of New York had become used to novelty, and Guston was stuck. He kept trying to solve an insoluble problem in a limited number of ways.[15] So even the catalogue essay for his own show conceded that Guston had reached an impasse. Guston retreated to Woodstock, New York, in 1966, and we can read this retreat as a pained acknowledgment of his predicament. Once removed to the countryside, Guston rethought and reworked his painting, as he had in 1948—by returning to its origins in drawing. In 1968 he started painting again.

So what *is* going on in the "new Gustons"? The differences between *New Place* and *City Limits* (probably the most famous painting in the Marlborough show in 1970) are as great as the similarities, and we have to ask how we can explain the transition from the claustrophobic narratives of the former to the great pink outdoors of the latter. The inherited language of formalism can help here. Guston's work between 1968 and 1970 attempted to bring his "homeless representation" (the expression is Greenberg's) back home. To understand what this might mean, we have to return to the unbearable tension Greenberg saw in "painterly" abstraction.

Greenberg borrowed the term *painterly* from the art historian Heinrich Wöllflin. The linear (which is both a style and an orientation) stresses static outlines and the physical limits of isolated objects. The painterly, on the other hand, emphasizes the flux of appearances and blurs outlines.[16] The two approaches represent "radically different interests in the world." The linear emphasizes solid figures and finite forms. The painterly investigates forms in action.[17] Guston's paintings in the Jewish Museum show attempted to square the circle between the linear (with its attempt to catch things as they truly are) and the painterly (with its subjection to time and contingency). They approached the linear through painterly means. The consciousness that this task was, by definition, impossible led to the pathos of "Faith, Hope and Impossibility" and the Piero essay. In such a light Guston's return to drawing after 1966 makes perfect sense. His works are linear in an uncomplicated way. They construct images from the outlines of objects, rather than from the inside, through erasure.

This formalist account of Guston's shift has some interesting implications. Guston's abstractions of the early and the middle 1960s were meant to serve as diagrams of the spatial relations between ultimately indeterminate objects. These paintings meditated on *where* things should be, but, given the paintings' limited repertoire of rectangular shapes, they did not worry so much about *what* those things might be. Their compositions acknowledged the temporal processes of their creation by highlighting the ambiguities that erasure produced. When Guston returned to figuration—as in *City Limits*—he did not mark the instability of his images this way. Instead, he resorted to other techniques, which rendered his work more "literary," that is, more reliant on language and temporal succession.

In an interview before the Marlborough show in 1970, Guston said that painting revealed the elasticity of forms. He could begin painting a shoe, and its sole could turn into the moon. He might start painting the moon, and it would turn into a piece of bread.[18] Guston's earlier fascination with the passage of images through time and space had given way to the Surrealist practice of visual puns. After 1968 it becomes hard to decide just what you are looking at but in a different way than in *New Place*. In one of his poetic responses to Guston's work, Clark Coolidge played up the semantic ambiguity of this strategy: "A book like a brick loaf. How to/read it?"[19] Three interpretations of the same object: book, brick, and loaf. Two different interpretations of Coolidge's lines: Is he asking how we read the book or how we read the image? Of course, he is asking both at the same time and reenacts in words what Guston enacts in his work. Guston's books did look like bricks, his buildings like books, and his heads like coffee cups.[20]

Sometimes the pun is carried out verbally as well as visually. In *Paw* (1968) a heavily shadowed and hairy hand, a lighter pink against an even more luxuriously pink background, draws a line with what looks like a stick. It might not be a stick, though. It could just as easily (and even more credibly) be a pencil, pen, quill, or brush. The line it sketches might also be nothing more than the shadow that the hand and wrist cast on the ground. The title of the painting points to both the demotic ("Get your paws offa me!") and the evolutionary. What Guston painted here is not clear. It could be a sophisticated primate, an artist, or a thug. Perhaps it is all these at once.

A similar play with semantic indeterminacy can be seen in *Cher-*

ries (1976). These cherries, portrayed in an ungainly lineup that resembles the apostles at the Last Supper, look like a bomb in a cartoon. The painting really depicts cherry bombs. It is a rebus and a rather silly one at that. Like the old Gestalt drawing of the duck that is also a rabbit, Guston's visual puns unfold in a temporal succession that never quite comes to an end because only one aspect is perceptible at any one time. Whereas Guston had previously represented the temporal process of discovering images by giving his lowering objects rather ambiguous contours, he now shifted the onus of this process to the spectator.[21]

The paintings of the Jewish Museum show of 1966 tried to achieve the linear through painterly means, and the works of the 1970 show approached the painterly through linear means. This schematization, though, does not do credit to the way that Guston worked through the tension between the painterly and the linear by pushing each to an extreme. Guston wanted to show stasis and flux, isolated object and the relation between objects. To play with Greenberg's terminology: the Marlborough works were "postlinear representations." Guston's cross-pollination of the painterly and the linear was a hybrid of his own brand of Abstract Expressionism and his own idiosyncratic understanding of Pop. While Guston rejected the purity and exclusiveness that he associated with the New York School, he could not accept the deskilling of the painter's task that he saw in Pop, Minimalism, and Conceptual art. He could not accept their elevation of the artist's "preexecutive" decisions—those decisions that come before the creation of the work of art—at the expense of traditional craft.

Guston's works of the late sixties and seventies register his complex response to Pop and represent his attempt to effect a rapprochement between painterly touch and Pop's "impurities." Elaine de Kooning remembered Guston saying, "Oh, Warhol, he's like giving a Jewish kid a hot pork sandwich on the day of his bar mitzvah."[22] Guston, who was never averse to repeating a good line, used it slightly differently on Thomas Hess. In a 1974 review Hess noted Guston's "comically intense hate-love for the blunt ironic realism of Pop Art" and mentioned how Guston had likened all Pop art (not just Warhol's) to feasting on pork after a Yom Kippur service.[23]

If Guston, a nonobservant Jew, could imagine Pop as a temptingly forbidden ham sandwich or a pork banquet, it was not because he was fascinated by Pop's subject matter. Dore Ashton reports that Guston ended a diatribe against the Pop artists by saying, "What they paint about just doesn't interest me."[24] At no point in his later work does Guston seem at all seduced by the Pop tendency to reproduce mass-produced cultural signs or to represent media representations. Nor is he interested in the industrial methods (silkscreens, airbrushes, and so on) used by the Pop artists. His thick application of paint and his emphasis on brushwork signal his difference from Pop.

Guston did not want to give up the painterly brushstroke. This mark of the craftsman's hand was, of course, a heavily burdened and burdensome aspect of Abstract Expressionism. It was easily parodied and thus called into question, but in its time it had stood as the last vestige of unalienated labor. Guston's friend Meyer Schapiro defended abstraction in the late 1950s. He argued that because paintings and sculptures were the last handmade objects, they constituted, "more passionately than ever before, the occasion of spontaneity or intense feeling."[25] In a world that seemed overwhelmed by mass production, the brushstroke, the application of paint, the trace of the painter's movement all showed that Abstract Expressionism was the last refuge of authentic unexploited personal expression. Guston was still voicing this opinion in 1966, when he asked whether it was still possible to create in America. Art, he said, was "the only thing left in our industrial society where an individual alone can make something with not just his own hands, but brains, imagination, heart maybe."[26] Guston's daughter, Musa Mayer, remembers that in the mid-1960s Guston despaired "over the selling of art, over the slick depersonalized gloss—not only of pop art, but of minimalism as well—that was taking center stage in New York." Art was no longer about struggle. It had become marketing.[27] As Benjamin Buchloh has noted, by the time Guston expressed his despair, the primacy of the studio "had been irreversibly replaced by an aesthetic of production and consumption."[28]

Guston mistrusted the art of the mid-1960s because he disliked the implications of the depersonalized industrial sheen of its surfaces, the absence of the artist's trace. He also disliked the emphasis on choice, not creation, that seemed to animate so much avant-garde work of the period. Guston could not stomach what Brian O'Doherty in 1964 called the avant-garde's modish "total abnegation of the self." O'Doherty's account shows how far things had come in the seven years that separated his article from Schapiro's. Vanguard art, O'Doherty wrote, had become "anti-spontaneous, its motifs logical, measurable, reproducible." The artist as artist had come to be ignored as "presumably unimportant."[29] In the face of all this Guston's paintings maintained the distinction between the handmade, personally expressive work and the anonymity of the mass product. When Guston summoned comics to his aid, he called up the visually distinctive, thematically quirky older strips of the teens, twenties, and thirties.

Guston's Marlborough show should have made perfect sense to its viewers and to the critics. After all, it showed precisely the air of independence that Charlotte Lichtblau saw in the New York art scene in the fall of 1970. But not everyone shared Lichtblau's sense that, for the first time in the twentieth century, artists were free to choose, that they were not governed by the imperatives of school and movement. While some critics—most notably Lawrence Alloway in the *Nation*—wrote favorably of the Marlborough show, some other very prominent ones did not. And, evidently, the opening night of the Marlborough show was unpleasant. One colleague from the 1950s reportedly asked Guston, "Why did you have to go and ruin everything?" Guston's wife, Musa McKim, noted in her diary that "P. said Lee Krasner hadn't spoken to him at the gallery; had told someone that the work was embarrassing."[30] More telling, and personally more devastating, Guston's long friendship with Morton Feldman ended in an instant. Guston asked the composer what he thought of a picture, and Feldman said, "Well, let me just look at it another minute." And that was that. Looking back, Feldman wrote that it was "extremely sad that we broke up because of style." In October 1970 Feldman could not get beyond the high modernist valorization of abstraction.[31] The Marlborough show must have seemed to him like an inexplicable regression, if not an outright betrayal.[32]

The three most visible reviews were negative. For all their differences Hilton Kramer, the furious scold of the *New York Times;* Robert Hughes, critic for the middlebrow journal *Time;* and Robert Pincus-Witten, writing for the leading art magazine of the time, *Artforum,* all agreed that something was distinctly wrong with Guston's show, although they disagreed about what that something actually was.

In an acidly personal attack on Guston, Kramer double-damned the artist for being both ingratiating and behind the times. No doubt referring to Guston's relatively late conversion to abstraction, Kramer accused the painter of having capitalized on other people's risks and revolutions, for being "one of those painters fated to serve a taste instead of creating one." But this time around Guston had gotten it wrong. The taste he was serving had already run its course. Claiming that Guston had now adopted the guise of "an urban primitive," Kramer argued that no one had been taken in by this ruse, except perhaps Guston himself, "who is so out-of-touch with contemporary realities that he still harbors the illusion his 'act' will not be recognized as such." In the end Kramer indicted Guston on four counts. His work was insincere and out of date. It aimed to please, and—worst of all—it failed to please.[33]

Less vitriolic (but no less critical), Robert Hughes's review in *Time* agreed that Guston's work suffered from anachronism. But Hughes felt that its intent, not its style, was outmoded. Hughes argued that it was "a little late in the century to mount an entire exhibition of the Ku Klux Klan." The Klan, Hughes maintained, was no longer a real force in American politics. More to the point, though, the show made it look as if Guston had "flipped back" to the late 1930s, "those remote days when it was still believed that political comment could give art relevance."[34] Like Kramer, Hughes double-damned the paintings. Guston had devoted the show to an irrelevant subject (a point that, for Harold Rosenberg, counted in Guston's favor).[35] What is more, Hughes wrote that painting had become "a clumsy way of reporting a society as turbulent and racked as this." Guston's paintings might be "sumptuously painted" and "occasionally moving," but they were "as simple-minded" as the bigotry they attacked.[36] Hughes was kinder to Guston than Kramer. The *Time* critic did not accuse the artist of smarmy insincerity. Rather, he wrote Guston off as a nostalgist.

In the most insightful of the negative reviews, Robert Pincus-Witten argued that Guston's subject matter was really secondary and that Guston was chiefly interested in solving outmoded compositional problems. The nostalgia that Guston seemed to express for old comic strips—particularly for Bill Holman's *Smokey Stover*—was "still about sensitive patches and Abstract Expressionist all-over." So Guston was not telling stories. He was fighting an older battle about the relation of different parts of the canvas.[37] For Pincus-Witten the weakness of the paintings lay quite literally on the surface, in the contradiction between the self-conscious high-style application of paint ("the altitude of the facture") and the "baseness of the humor."[38] The contradiction undid the ideal of compositional unity the paintings seemed to endorse.

At first blush these three reviews of Guston's Marlborough show do not seem to overlap. Kramer doubted Guston's sincerity and showed contempt for the painter's willingness to please. He argued that Guston was nothing more than a newly minted neoprimitivist. Hughes claimed that political painting was no longer tenable, in large part because the movies did politics so much better. Pincus-Witten felt that Guston's aesthetics were out of date and that the paintings' internal disjunctions undermined those aesthetics. Nevertheless, the family resemblances in Kramer, Hughes, and Pincus-Witten are strong.

They all agreed that valuable artistic activity is marked by innovation. They also agreed that artistic innovation needs historical justification, a place in an accepted and acceptable historical narrative. If innovation is not historically necessary—if it comes too late or does not seem like the logical next step—then it is regressive or merely idiosyncratic. Style can serve as a good gauge of the new, though style was obviously less important for Hughes than it was for Kramer, Pincus-Witten, or Feldman.

These assumptions testified to a loose but insistent vanguardism that owed much to what Caroline Jones has called the "Greenberg effect," the general currency of Greenberg's ideas even among those who seemed to oppose him.[39] The stories that different critics told about modernism could differ—for some Picasso might be the founding father; for others, Marcel Duchamp—but they shared the sense that the progress of art was a logical working-through of formal problems. Guston's Marlborough show did not meet these vanguardist criteria. While Guston's switch from abstraction to figuration marked a new step for Guston, Kramer, Hughes, and Pincus-Witten all felt that it did not mark a new stage in the history of art. In fact, they argued that Guston's figurative work signaled a historical step backward.

Their adverse judgments of Guston's works contained important insights, although not in the way the critics intended. Kramer's dismissal of Guston's desire to court his audience points to something very real. Guston had recognized that the transgressive nature of Pop went beyond its formal license. It really *was* a pork chop in the synagogue. Pop was liberating because it promised a closer relation to its viewers than Abstract Expressionism had ever allowed. For the established critics of the early 1960s, one of the greatest scandals of Pop art was that it cozied up to its public. "Audience" had been a tricky notion for American defenders of the avant-garde since World War II because the audience could no longer be associated with an uneducated and ungrateful bourgeoisie. Rosenberg had realized this in the 1950s when he maintained that art no longer had a general audience. While the notion of a general audience had always been a myth, the public for postwar art consisted of "a sum of shifting groupings, each with its own mental focus."[40] Pop offended the specialized audience of art professionals, many of whom had staked their reputations on the importance of Abstract Expressionism.[41] They generated angry reviews in no small part because, as far as they could tell, the Pop vanguard did *not* want to tweak that fictive general public.

A number of critics assumed that an apparent lack of anti-bourgeois sentiment meant that the Pop artists were celebrating the status quo. Some critics went as far as to accuse the artists of practicing the aesthetic equivalent of Goldwaterism. A nicely virulent editorial in *Arts* accused the Pop artists of sharing with a philistine middle class a "vain, almost boastful insistence upon its own cultural limitations."[42] Between 1962 and 1968 this sentiment also colored the editorial polemics against Pop in *Art News*, which were clearly meant to protect abstraction as the only truly avant-garde course worth pursuing. The nature of this polemic was nicely illustrated by Thomas Hess's attacks on the "vanguard audience." This audience had replaced the avant-garde artist, he argued, and it was driven by a relentless "appetite for novelties, for art as an object of conversation, a rung in the social ladder, a cheap investment." Culturally naive, stunningly ignorant, and politically conservative, the vanguard audience ignored "the crisis content of modern art." Instead of understanding the alienation that modernism had expressed, the audience invited the artist to dinner. These "arriviste" collectors were really celebrating themselves and their wealth and not the genius of art. Their enthusiasm reflected their narcissism, and they "cowered" in their "trim apartments with specially low ceilings among the latest junk."[43] Hess eventually gave up this tone of class condescension and wrote that holding up collectors like "the Sculls for special ridicule merely seems an unpleasant form of a most unpleasant snobbism."[44] But his attack on the "vanguard audience" had become an increasingly standard feature of the reviews of established (and antagonistic) critics, such as Rosenberg, Greenberg, and Kramer.

The snobbism that underlay Hess's critique of the "vanguard audience" rested on a romanticized nostalgia for a recent artistic past when the serious modernist pitted his works against the muddle-headed middle class. The critics who mourned the death of a meritocracy based on taste and not money were also protecting their hard-won cultural authority, an authority they had earned defending a high modernist version of Abstract Expressionism. They had defined the New York School in terms of its opposition to the tastes and preoccupations of the bourgeoisie.[45] Pop art seemed to undermine their position on every front. In a historical twist many established critics found themselves in the odd position of having to attack the public in the name of aesthetic purity because artworks no longer wanted to.

Pop's unpainterly use of paint seemed to get rid of expression—that telltale drip—that had come to look like a cliché. At the same time its subject matter returned painting directly to the realm of appetite and consumption.[46] In this way Pop appeared to pander to inferior taste. In the end, though, it had not really succumbed to philistinism. It had redefined it. Pop did not reward the philistines by providing them with the ready-made emotions that Greenberg had ascribed to kitsch. One constant complaint about early Pop was that its emotions were so cool that its positions were practically illegible. And Pop did not reject the philistine. It did not make its own formal concerns inaccessible by limiting its aesthetic rewards to the chosen few. By the same token, because it appeared to open the door to everyone, Pop troubled the principles of division—based on style, subject matter, and audience—that had been central to the self-definition of the New York art world in the 1950s. Nevertheless, Pop still maintained the privileges of the avant-garde. It was new and it was provocative.

Guston took up this challenge. He worried his style and changed his subject matter so that his work could become more accessible while maintaining its painterly quality. He did not seek to reject the viewer or split the audience into philistines and cognoscenti. As early as 1966 Guston noted that Abstract Expressionism demanded an unreasonable amount of work from the viewer. It asked its audience to imagine the links between the artist's past, present, and future paintings in order to figure out what precisely is at stake in them.[47] In 1977 Guston repeated this charge by pointing out that the decorum of post-Cubist painting required too much collaboration between the artist and "the all-too-willing viewer."[48] Guston felt that abstract art was self-congratulatory in its exclusions. His appeal for an extended aesthetic franchise worked itself out as the ingratiating quality that Kramer so disliked in Guston's painting.

Guston's figurations of the late 1960s dissolved many fierce dichotomies that drove the New York art world. A certain reductive aspiration seemed to unite postpainterly abstractionists, Minimalists, and conceptualists, who agreed that the most advanced works of art aspired to the zero degree of art.[49] Of course, the paths these reductions actually took were remarkably dissimilar and could include almost anything, from a formalist emphasis on the "opacity of the medium" in the individual saleable work to an antiformalist fascination with the uncommodifiable act of the artist. In 1970, when Guston dismissed all this with his gruff and provocative claim that he had gotten "sick and tired of all that Purity" and "wanted to tell Stories," he was explicitly embracing storytelling at a time when the term *literary* was still used as an insult.[50] What is more, Guston justified his embrace of figuration by appealing to the vagaries of his personal taste and not to art historical necessity. He thus opened himself to the charge of being merely arbitrary, although he was in fact intensely aware of his place in art history and in the New York art world of the late 1960s. Yet he willingly (if defensively) assumed the guise of arbitrariness because he did not accept the art historical narratives of his critics. Against the relative simplicity of avant-garde genealogies, he presented a complex example of the way artists take positions in relation not only to their past but also to their present. Guston meant this when he said at the Philadelphia panel a few years earlier that the continuities of art were forced by the constant adjustment of "impurities." In this view the history of painting consisted of strings of contingent stops and starts. It flatly denied the narratives (of which Greenberg's was surely the most influential) in which art developed through a set of necessary moves toward a foreordained end. Guston explicitly reversed the terms of this narrative in a letter to Rosenberg in 1977 in which Guston claimed that the art "which accepts its own limitations of its means" becomes "elegant and conventional." It has to and thus loses the "rawness, the inchoate, the heretofore unsaid and unseen of experience." Guston then restated his conviction that art struggles with its impurities. It "needs to continue, strangely enough, by denying its own means."[51] In Guston's view art maintains its dynamism only by courting the external. Given such an argument, subject matter—for formalists, merely an occasion for experiments with the medium—became all important.

Thinking Thoughtlessness

Guston's critical fortunes reached their lowest ebb in the four years after the Marlborough exhibition in 1970. He left the gallery in 1972 and did not show in New York until 1974, at which point he started receiving largely positive reviews. Why this reversal? It would be tempting to cast Guston as a prophet, as Peter Schjeldahl would in 1984.[1] But it would not be accurate to say that the reviewers had to catch up to Guston, because Guston's work itself changed during the seventies.

In his review of the Marlborough show, Lawrence Alloway claimed that Guston was no longer a painter of the "I" or the "thou" but of the "them."[2] In 1978 Roberta Smith argued that Guston's paintings of the early seventies were public, unlike his later private works.[3] While commentators have generally assumed that Guston's pictures of the Hoods were political, how they were specifically topical is not altogether clear. Although the Klansmen still served as bogeymen in the late 1960s, they had ceased to bear, as Robert Hughes and Harold Rosenberg noted at the time, any real political weight.[4] What is more, Guston's Hoods were hardly frightening. One need only compare the enormous hands and elongated figures of Guston's 1930 sketch for *Conspirators* to the dumpy, klutzy, and ultimately silly Klansmen of the Marlborough show to see just how fuzzy the message had become. The rags-and-tatters members of the Klan owed as much to the commedia dell'arte as they did to political reaction. They were also remarkably superficial. As Kenneth Baker pointed out in 1974, there are no faces behind the masks of the Hoods.[5] Their masks *are* their faces. This is very different from, and has a different effect than, *Red Eyes* (1969), a painting of a Hood whose eyes peer *through* the mask.

Because these paintings' specific references remain obscure, it is worthwhile to compare them with Gustons whose political content is clear. In the summer of 1971 the painter produced a series of cartoons about Nixon (plate 3).[6] The series, *Poor Richard*, charts Nixon's course from Whittier to the White House and on to China, although Nixon's historic trip to Beijing was still in the planning stages when Guston composed the series in August 1971. The Hoods turn up in a series of drawings that begins with Nixon—his nose reworked as a large flaccid penis and his jowls imaged as a pair of testicles—mugging for the camera with three groups of carefully selected members of "the silent majority." Guston then presents Nixon and his allies John Mitchell and Spiro Agnew as Hoods in a slapstick burlesque. After Agnew gets bonked by a coconut, and Nixon and Agnew peer into each other's empty head, the hoods get thrown into a garbage can.

While the appearance of the Klan might refer to the thinly veiled race-baiting of the presidential race of 1968, the comic to-and-fro between Nixon and Agnew remains murky. And that is the odd part of *Poor Richard.* Beyond the scabrous depiction of Nixon's famous nose, Guston's caricatures exhibit an odd indecisiveness. They lack the specific bite of ready reference. This is noteworthy, because the previous year had provided plenty of reasons for bitter satire. Nixon had fought a hardball partisan campaign in the midterm elections of 1970. He had authorized the bombing of Cambodia, had pardoned Lt. William Calley, the convicted war criminal, and had promised a "Vietnamization" that never occurred. This brief résumé does not mention Nixon's economic policies, his civil rights difficulties, or his foreign policy initiatives. *Poor Richard* depicts none of this.

To understand what *Poor Richard* leaves out, you need only look at Guston's provocation for the cartoons—*Our Gang*, the novel that his friend Philip Roth was writing during that summer. Roth's Nixon is unambiguously evil. Here he is, staging yet another comeback, campaigning to be the Devil in Hell:

> I think I speak for all opportunists when I say that Satan has been a constant source of inspiration to us from time immemorial, in good times and in bad. . . . But let me make one thing perfectly clear. Much as I respect and admire his lies, I don't think that lies are anything to stand on. I think they are something to build on.[7]

Roth picked up on Nixon's cadences and favorite turns of phrase. By mocking Nixon's sanctimonious, self-pitying manipulations of the truth, Roth created the Nixon of liberal nightmares: a conspiratorial, self-serving, and hypocritical liar.

Guston's Nixon is quite different. Guston appears to have been most interested in Nixon at play. A surprising number of cartoons show Nixon relaxing on Key Biscayne, and more than half are devoted to Nixon's imagined/imaginary trip to Asia. (There are no Chinese in Nixon's hallucinatory China.) What is more, the loosely organized narrative devolves completely after the China sequence into a series of visual puns, in which one thing is transformed into another. Nixon's and Agnew's heads become broken statuary dotting a desert. Key Biscayne is transformed into a floating toilet. Nixon's nose turns into a hamburger, and Kissinger metamorphoses into a pot pie. There is an Agnew sponge cake and a Nixon cookie. Given Nixon's protean ability to remake himself, Guston's games make a certain kind of sense. And it also makes sense that Guston's fascination with the elasticity of form should cause him to look at Nixon this way. But it is stunning that Guston, a skilled caricaturist, would ignore Nixon's numerous tics. Guston's Nixon has the body of a slim young man. Gone are the forward thrust of Nixon's head, his painfully hunched shoulders, and the hammy triumphalism of his victory signs.

At first blush, then, *Poor Richard* does not make sense. But Guston's fascination with a vacationing Nixon provides the link between the paintings of the Hoods in the late 1960s and the drawings of Nixon in 1971. Guston had described his Klansmen in terms of the very evil that in retrospect they seem to lack. He said he was fascinated by the idea of evil and "rather like Isaac Babel who had joined the Cossacks," Guston "almost tried to imagine" that he was living with the Klan. "What would it be like to be evil?" he asked. What would it be like "to plan and to plot."[8] In the paintings of the Marlborough show, Guston's Hoods might have been planning and plotting, but they mostly waited around or cruised along in cars. They were depicted in their off-hours. Guston painted evil smoking, hanging out, and talking.

Guston's reference to Isaac Babel, the Soviet Jewish writer who hailed from Odessa, the hometown of Guston's parents, is revealing. Babel's Cossacks are not particularly evil. While they are indeed violent, impulsive, illiterate, and anti-Semitic, Babel was careful to grant them a primitive "natural" nobility and a remarkable incapacity for lying. He admired the Cossacks, albeit from a distance. The pathos and the humor of Babel's *Red Cavalry* stories derive from the narrator's frustrated attempts to emulate the Cossacks. As Babel was quite unequivocal on this score, Guston meant something quite specific when he called his Hoods and Babel's Cossacks evil.

They are not evil in any traditional way, that is, out of an excess of hubris or desire. Rather, they are evil in a distinctly modern everyday way. They are banal. In this they appear to owe much to Hannah Arendt's notorious description of Adolf Eichmann, the engineer of the Final Solution.[9] Eichmann presented a problem for Arendt because his "deeds were monstrous, but the doer . . . was quite ordinary, commonplace, and neither demonic nor monstrous."[10] In *Eichmann in Jerusalem* Arendt presented Eichmann as a ludicrous buffoon, constantly at war with the German language and hopelessly lost in a haze of hackneyed expressions. Hardly a figure of either genius or will, he was depicted as a resentful, self-pitying, petty bourgeois bureaucrat who happened to have a particular talent for organization. This *Spiessbürger* was a painfully ordinary man who suffered from a very particular, very ordinary kind of thoughtlessness. His inability to speak German properly was, according to Arendt, "closely connected with an inability to *think*, namely, to think from the standpoint of somebody else."[11] Eichmann's narcissistic self-enclosure crowded everybody out with cliché. In Arendt's opinion Eichmann's great crime was that he ignored the irreplaceable humanity of others.

Arendt's report on the Eichmann trial was famously controversial. Some of her judgments were unnecessarily harsh and some of her facts disputable. More important, though, readers mistook Arendt's argument as an exculpation of Eichmann. These readers—and many who expressed an opinion without ever reading her book—did not recognize the fury behind the cold irony of Arendt's densely literate and literary style. As Dagmar Barnouw has pointed out, Arendt's use of indirect quotation got her into trouble because it was taken as evidence that she had taken Eichmann's side. Given the argument that thoughtlessness entails the inability to see things from the other person's point of view, it should have been clear that Arendt's book was hardly a defense of Eichmann. It was, rather, an exercise in thought. It marked the attempt to think *about* Eichmann—to think from his point of view.[12] The naked derision with which Arendt treated the man should have made it obvious that she never condoned his point of view.

Arendt argued that to think about contemporary evil was to think about thoughtlessness. Such thinking would have to mimic the very thoughtlessness it analyzed and by definition rejected. It would undergo banality in order to go beyond it. But the danger with such a meditation on evil is that it can be mistaken for evil itself. What is even worse, though, as Arendt indicated, is that such evil might not be recognizable. No longer demonic or willful, modern evil—the crime of thoughtlessness—is laughable.

Evil, then, is self-regard without self-reflection, guilt without consciousness of guilt. Guston's Nixon, like his Hoods, is culpable without ever realizing it. Guston drew Nixon as Nixon imagined himself—young, slim, ramrod straight, a regular guy. Hence the insouciance of his play, of his ability to play. Guston's Nixon is different from Roth's. Although Roth tried to catch Nixon in his own words, his Nixon knows that what he is doing is wrong. Part of the humor of the book derives from Nixon's attempt to conceal from himself, as well as from others, his awareness of his shenanigans. Guston's Nixon is completely insulated from any such awareness. He is evil precisely because he is blind to his own hypocrisy. He is incapable of self-analysis.

Guston's presentation of the Hoods shows the artistic possibilities of such thoughtlessness. *A Day's Work* (1970; plate 4) depicts a room. On the back wall two rectangles stand in for pictures. The center of the painting is dominated by an improbable stack of Guston's typical junk: shoes, boots (one pair attached to cuffed legs), some red and apparently dripping limbs, vertical pieces of wood, and a "two by four with nails in it" that Thomas Hess mistook for a typewriter.[13] When Guston retold the story of Hess's mistake, he made an interesting slip. He claimed that the nails were red, and they are not red. But they should be, because of the prevalence of red in the work and because they are most likely meant as weapons.

In the foreground of the painting stand two Hoods. One faces away. His shoulder is stained red, and he holds a stogey in two bloody red fingers. The other is presented in three-quarter profile, and he wears his red stains in front. The shoulders of a third figure, who has been painted out, form part of a table that itself seems like a recollection of a Matisse interior. It is not clear whether the painting presents a summary of an ordinary workday of severing and stacking limbs and shoes. Perhaps these two guys are kicking back after a hard day of depredation. If this is the case, the most effective part of the painting might be its casual reduction of murder to mere work. The atrocities hinted at here become nothing more than a job, which is unpleasant in the way that all work can be said to be unpleasant or merely unconscious ("all in a day's work").

The faces of the two Hoods are unreadable beyond a kind of animal perplexity. Their eyes are slits that resemble the windows in Guston's paintings of exteriors. In *Outskirts* (1969) Guston made this equation between windows and eyes quite clear. What renders this rather trite analogy interesting—if not a little scary—is that the windows/eyes look like the writing in his paintings of books, where the characters are nothing more than vertical lines. These eyes have been blacked out. If they are the windows of the soul, that soul is blank.

If *A Day's Work* shows a deadpan version of any equally deadpan and banal evil, the limits of its subject become clear in *Scared Stiff* (1970), in which a Hood sits in a red chair before a red square table, in a room rendered claustrophobic by the apparent lowness of the ceiling. He is daubed with red, and his red hand holds Guston's iconic cigar. A large-scale red hand that looks like Mickey Mouse's glove because of the three lines on its back dominates the center of the painting. Its index finger points at the Hood. In 1977 Guston claimed that this painting shows a courtroom and that the Hood should be read as a defendant.[14] If this is the case, the moral status of the accusatory red hand is ambiguous because it appears to be as bloodstained as the Hood's. The title is also unclear, and again the defendant's eyes tell us nothing. Six gray-blue and black rounded forms seem to rise like clouds. They could be smoke from the stogey or thought balloons.

David Carrier has suggested that one of the great innovations of the cartoon is the word balloon, which externalizes thought and makes the "inner world of represented figures" transparent to the cartoon's readers.[15] Carrier argues that because of our lack of common reference, narrative painting has become illegible for modern audiences. It refers to stories that are no longer generally known.[16] The comic solves this problem by providing its own text and organizes its frames into temporal sequences. Guston, for all his apparent reliance on the tradition of American comics, stops just short of this. He does not actually use thought balloons, nor (except in *Poor Richard*) does he construct narrative *sequences*. Hence the problem of *Scared Stiff*. Without the title (and Guston's commentary) we would not recognize the story, and we could not attribute emotion—in this case, fear—to the Hood. We do not know if the title is to be read ironically. The affectless face of the Hood and the thought balloons, necessary but empty as smoke, mean that the "inner world" of the central figure is far from transparent. More likely, it has no inner world. Thus the painting's obscurities are not particularly productive. In this case blank thoughtlessness yields little.

Guston stopped painting the Hoods after 1972. By then he appears to have seen that he had reached a dead end. What is more— and this is speculation—a man as riven by doubt and as captivated by nuance as Guston would have found the banality of evil ultimately constricting, if only because it could yield neither depth nor nuance. So Guston shed the Hoods and thoughtlessness. He moved in another direction, one that the critics can help us understand, because Guston's new subject matter coincided with their interests, and his medium—painting—enjoyed a critical revival.

By the early 1970s the status and value of painting had become unclear. The September 1975 issue of *Artforum* was dedicated to this "crisis in painting." It was a decidedly downbeat issue. The cover gives a taste of its retrospective melancholic tone. Instead of a painting, pride of place was given to a Hans Namuth photograph of Jackson Pollock taken a good twenty-five years earlier. The main article was devoted to painters' responses to a rather loaded question: Is painting dead? "Those understood to be making 'the next inevitable step,'" the editors asserted, "now work with any material but paint."[17] The editors argued that the conflict between abstraction and representation had resulted in a rather tedious stalemate. Nevertheless, they were also ambivalent about the historical narrative they felt they were forced to use. The scare quotes around "the next inevitable step" indicate that they did not necessarily subscribe to the progressivist notion of art historical necessity that they relied on. When they pointed out that painting had become outmoded, precisely because "those understood to be" in the vanguard were not painters at all, the editors' use of the passive ("understood to be") betrayed their discomfort with high modernist tales of apostolic succession. They might have distrusted this story, but they were clearly unwilling to give it up. Only the veteran critic and painter Sidney Tillim pointed out the real oddity of the questionnaire, when he argued that while its politics were anti-Greenbergian, the reasoning behind it ultimately fell into the ultra-Greenbergian camp.[18]

Not surprisingly, most painters who responded reacted defensively, although they did not really dispute the editors' basic terms. Most repeated entrenched and outmoded apologies for their chosen medium. They appealed to the dignity of emotions or to the power of the individual imagination. They looked to painting's long history as a justification in itself or—somewhat irrelevantly—referred to the pleasures of actually painting. Alternatively, they called on the need for concerted aesthetic contemplation, a need that painting, it seemed, was particularly good at fulfilling.

The samizdat New York art journal *Art-Rite* turned Tillim's insight into satire. This was typical of the journal, whose tone, the editor Edit DeAk remembers, was new and decidedly irreverent: "It was unheard of to have a sense of humor at the time, or not to be talking about 'the problem' of art—the problem of this, the problem of that."[19] Accordingly, *Art-Rite* dismissed with its own parodic questionnaire the "problem" of painting that *Artforum* presented. *Art-Rite* claimed that *Artforum* was outmoded, arguing that "those understood to be making 'the next inevitable step' now work with any material but *Artforum*."[20] *Art-Rite*'s editors were poking fun at the deep editorial problems that *Artforum* had been suffering in the previous two years.[21] Their less esoteric meaning was also clear. Painting and painters were doing just fine. The mode of criticism represented by *Artforum* was what had become outmoded.

Even so, the articles in *Art-Rite* pretended that painting did not need a good solid defense. In *Artforum* Max Kozloff had blamed painting's waning mystique on both painters and critics. Kozloff maintained that the painters were most at fault because they tried to avoid expressiveness in what is essentially an expressive medium. Thus the critical rejection of painting was the direct result of the artists' own rejection of personal expression.[22] In a counterarticle in *Art-Rite*, Jeremy Gilbert-Rolfe attacked this notion. He did not agree that painting was essentially expressive. He did not buy what he considered to be the myth of heroic individualism that had been so important to the criticism of the fifties and the sixties.[23]

Gilbert-Rolfe argued that the choice was not between painting and not-painting but between an outdated expressive individualism and painting's drive toward self-criticism. This drive did not allow painting to achieve its essence, as in the formalist argument, but helped it shuck its ideologically suspect notions, such as expression itself.

Although arguments like Gilbert-Rolfe's would become the coin of the realm by the early eighties, the equation of painting and self-expression was still common in the late seventies. It served as the premise of Barbara Rose's polemical exhibition "American Painting: The Eighties" at the Grey Gallery in 1979. Drawing a healthy part of her argument from Richard Hennessy's defense of painting's sensuous and expressive superiority to photography in *Artforum*, Rose attacked the critical popularity of photography and championed the imagination, painter's touch, and legacy of Pollock.[24]

Painting might have been tied to expressiveness in the 1970s, but that did not mean that everyone agreed about what was being expressed. In an article in 1979, the year of Julian Schnabel's first New York show, Dupuy Warrick Reed argued that the painter had "a special talent for transforming emotion into a visible, material object, and attempts to communicate honesty and clarity directly."[25] Schnabel thus communicated not only emotion but also clarity. But whose emotion and whose clarity? Reed claimed that the feelings expressed in the paintings are not those of an individual but those of a "collective subjective."[26]

At the same time Anita Feldman was arguing that contemporary abstractions represented subjectivity through conflicts between figure and ground. She went on to write that "before it is a picture of anything, a painting is a representation of consciousness."[27] Again, though, the question remains: Whose consciousness? These critics (and I am taking them to be exemplary after a fashion) were not particularly rigorous in their methods or arguments, but their very lack of rigor points to the currency of the notion that painting was associated with subjectivity, however broadly defined. The return to painting in the late seventies marked (and here I am quoting Hal Foster) "a return to the values of craft and subjectivity, to the art object as original product and the artist as creative producer."[28] By 1980 critics of all stripes agreed that the restoration of painting was a done deal, although they disagreed about the desirability of such a restoration and the actual meaning of the works involved. Painting had indeed become its own "next inevitable step" despite the rather glum predictions of *Artforum* in 1975. The importance of "neo-Expressionism" in the first years of the 1980s (as well as the growth of similar movements, such as graffiti art) shows just how strong the identification of painting and subjectivity turned out to be.[29]

This rehabilitation of painting as a form of expression helps explain the revival of Guston's reputation after 1974. While Guston's stock rose in the middle and late seventies, the critics who came to praise him were not the ones who had attacked him in 1970, although Hilton Kramer had come around to a surprising, if very grudging, respect. More to the point, the terms of the argument had changed. Whereas reactions to the Marlborough show had concentrated on the discontinuities of Guston's career, the reviewers at mid-decade were more interested in tracing the continuities. And their discussions of form quickly shaded into an important emphasis on content.

Kenneth Baker reviewed the 1974 show when it first opened in Boston and noted that Guston's figurative paintings recalled the composition of the earlier abstract ones. The colors of the newer paintings also harked back to Guston's earlier work, but now the pinks and reds seemed to be "the colors of soreness."[30]

When this exhibition moved to New York, Thomas Hess and Lawrence Campbell also emphasized the links between the different stages of Guston's development.[31] While Noel Frackman noted the similarities between earlier and later Gustons, she was particularly taken with how Guston's works bravely represented the "foibles, fears, needs and passions that characterize the human species," a species that is "spiritually isolated in an alien world." For Frackman, Guston depicts "an existential world without salvation."[32]

This theme was sounded in other reviews as well, most memorably in John Russell's review for the *New York Times:* "It is as if the protagonist in Beckett's 'Krapp's Last Tape' had mislaid even the tape, and just lay there, holed up."[33] Beckett served as a reliable touchstone for Guston's reviewers in the late 1970s. Guston's friend Ross Feld wrote in 1976 that Guston's "stunning paintings" did not present "a message of utter reductive bleakness." They displayed "the totally scoured and therefore pristine hope of a few of the finest modern artists: Beckett's hope, Kierkegaard's."[34] On a similar note Peter Frank claimed that Guston's works portrayed "a Samuel Beckett world, the heads rolling around the desert terrain and facing each other expressionlessly."[35]

In 1970 Clark Coolidge had noted that Guston's Marlborough paintings looked "a lot like Crumb World."[36] Six years later the register had shifted from the counterculture to high culture, and R. Crumb's Mr. Natural had given way to *Endgame*. When Kay Larson argued in 1974 that Guston's later works bore no relation to the art historical mainstream, she was thinking primarily about style.[37] Roberta Smith wrote in 1978 that Guston's interest in subject matter gave his work a relevance for "a decade which seems distinguished by its dearth of neatly labeled art movements," and that content had replaced style precisely because there were no movements that constituted an avant-garde, nor any movements that constituted the mainstream.[38] This shift from style to content was the result, in no small part, of a relative decline of formalist narratives.

By the end of the seventies even the formal elements that had seemed arbitrary to Guston's critics in 1970 had become strengths or historical necessities. In 1977 Hilton Kramer was willing to accept both that Guston was a beautiful painter and that the structure of his paintings was authoritative. But the split between form and content in Guston's work—what Robert Pincus-Witten seven years earlier had noted as the discrepancy between the "altitude of the facture and the baseness of the humor"—was still too much for Kramer.[39] On the other hand, Carrie Rickey argued in 1979 that the disjunctions in Guston's works were exemplary. She claimed that Guston was in fact a pioneer, because he had predicted that in the future some artists "will be remembered as great formalists, but those who set out to be formalists will be dismissed entirely." Rickey praised "his peculiar combinations of grotesque subject matter set against lyrical brushwork," his "carefully composed canvases of decomposing and rusty matter." She singled out precisely those formal incongruities that Pincus-Witten and Kramer had found so problematic: "Guston, no stranger to contradiction, successfully pits content against form."[40]

Within a year Rickey was willing to go for broke. In 1980 she maintained quite flatly that "Guston's career is the history of American painting this century."[41] In the year of his death Guston had become Modern Art.

The shift in Guston criticism registers a shift in Guston's own work. Guston really had moved from Crumb world to Beckett world when his figures took off their hoods. To see what was at stake, compare *Bad Habits* (1970; plate 5) to *Head and Bottle* (1975; plate 6). *Bad Habits* presents a typical Guston interior. A curtain is drawn across the window, and a single bulb in the center of the painting appears to light the scene. A large bottle whose whiteness has bled onto a red table dominates the foreground. Another smaller bottle stands on the right. Butts lie on both the left and right sides of table. Again the painting depicts two Hoods. One, apparently closer to the viewer, is speckled with red and holds a whip, although it is not clear whether he is whipping himself or preparing to strike the other figure, and it is hard, therefore, to decide how the title relates to the painting. The Hood with the whip might be a penitent. Perhaps self-flagellation is a self-destructive source of pleasure, like smoking and drinking. It might signal atonement for a bad habit or a bad habit in itself.

Head and Bottle (1975) describes a clearer emotional relationship between the human figures and the objects of their desire than does *Bad Habits*. A huge ruddy head, which is all eye and blue unshaven jowl (and Guston's receding hairline), stares down at the bottom of an empty bottle that is lying on a table along with both a paintbrush and a small flattened roll of canvas. The painting emphasizes the single staring eye. The head has no mouth, because in this reduced universe everything passes through the eye. The furrowed brow indicates that the head is bothered by the emptiness of the bottle. The sheer hugeness of that head (as opposed to the centrality and size of the bottle in *Bad Habits*) ensures that its fixed attention serves as the subject of the painting.

Guston's paintings became more baroque in the early 1970s, because the rhetorical expressiveness of facial features did so much work. The firmness of the figures' outlines (its "linear" quality) pointed to an increased literalness of all aspects of the painting so that the mental was rendered as a tangible object. Desire was made concrete so that the psychological, physical, and temporally distinct are all made equally present. This new aspect of Guston's work is clear in *Painting, Smoking, Eating* (1973; plate 7), in which one of Guston's noseless heads lies smoking in a bed that runs horizontally across the canvas. On his chest, in vivid black outline, is a plate of French fries dripping a particularly lurid red ketchup. Next to the bed, facing the viewer, are two brush pots, whose mass is implied through shading and contour lines. Behind the bed we see Guston's familiar clutter: a bare lightbulb counterpoised by the pull of a window blind; piles of shoes whose soles press up against the picture plane. A hand, holding a paintbrush, is caught in the act of painting those soles on a canvas. The ghost of another blind-pull in the center seems to be a relic of erasure.

If this erasure points to the painting's own immediate past, a number of spectral indications point to the future. Several shoes, like the brush pots and the fries, are outlined in black and colored in a stronger, more vivid, red. Like the hand, which reaches out at an odd angle, the other shoes, the canvas, and the lightbulb are outlined more lightly in red and are colored in pink. How to understand this odd appearance of aerial perspective in a rather tightly claustrophobic indoor scene? In 1977 Guston interpreted the painting in a rather odd way: "There is a guy lying in bed eating a bunch of French fries, imagining this pile of stuff above him."[42] This is a peculiar claim because the guy in the bed has not yet touched the fries, while he *does* appear to be painting. Guston seems to have used the aerial perspective to denote what the painter is imagining, not what is happening.

There is no reason to favor Guston's interpretation. After all, one of the peculiarities of English is that the participles of the painting's title are elastic. They encompass different tenses and moods. (I was eating, I am eating, I will be eating, I might have been eating, I wish I were eating, etc.) On the visual evidence of *Painting, Smoking, Eating* it is hard, if not impossible, to tell what is going on and when. The figure in bed is definitely smoking. This certainty is based on the firmness of the cigarette's outline and its darker red. Is the reclining figure painting at the same time? The strange angle of the hand and the lighter outline of both the hand and the canvas suggest that it is not. The figure is either thinking of painting (as Guston claims) or thinking of what he will be painting. In this case perspective translates temporal difference into spatial illusion. This is a visual way of depicting the ability of participles to act as either verbs or nouns. They can move from being actions to being things. In fact, they turn actions into things.

Then there are those fries. They are also irrefutably *there*, as much a thumpingly physical fact as anything else in the painting. But we have no idea if and when they will be eaten. The painter's eye looks away from the plate. No hand moves toward it, however distractedly. It would be a mistake to want to reduce the painting to the literal rendition of a scene—a reduction that the painting itself will not allow. The title is reticent about what tense and what mood to apply.

Between 1970 and 1974 Guston shifted his attention from superficial and thoughtless evil by investigating the vagaries of desire, guilt, and suffering. In so doing he met his critics halfway. What makes these later paintings so striking and so ambiguous is their apparent lack of depth. But this lack of depth signals something new. Nothing is left on the "inside." Emotion, desire, and fantasy get externalized and are physically ramified. By 1974 both mental and physical stuff hangs out on the surface of Guston's paintings, pressed up hard against the picture plane.

In this light the rather frequent comparisons with Beckett and the critics' recourse to existential terminology after the publication of Dore Ashton's monograph in 1976 make sense. In an untitled painting of 1980, a bandaged head looks up the incline of a detritus-strewn hill with a rather set air of determination. We can see in this more than a touch of Beckett's humor and the bleak resilience of the famous end of *The Unnameable:* "I'll never know, in the silence you don't know, you must go on, I can't go on, I'll go on."[43] Beckett expresses a grotesque vision of the Cartesian split—a extraordinarily voluble clarity tied to physical infirmity and repulsiveness that also marks Guston's work.[44] Beckett's humor frequently comes from the incongruity between a dispassionate distanced diction and the rough-and-tumble grossness of what is being described. It pits a fiercely lucid consciousness against the intractability of the flesh.

Guston shares this slapstick sense of the physical. But Beckett's work is adamantly *not* autobiographical.[45] Beckett's existential quality derives from his ability to elide all the particularities of place, history, and personal identity. Nothing is left but the situation of the naked, catastrophically limited consciousness caught in elusive, frequently elemental relations with unnamed others. This consciousness is locked in either an extended extensive space or the bitterly claustrophobic emptiness of a room, skull, or body. Beckett reduces his characters to their minimum—in the most extreme cases to the merest flicker of memory or consciousness.

Guston's work, on the other hand, is clearly autobiographical. He grants his figures his eyes, his hair, his bad habits, and his métier. He refers to his immediate family. He paints figures of his wife after her stroke. Guston's reductions lie elsewhere—in figures leveled down to faces with neither nose nor mouth and in the constant repetition of common objects.

Guston's tragicomic view of the way that consciousness is moored to the inertial weight of the decaying body and its desires does indeed find a kindred spirit, if not inspiration, in Beckett. But it also owes a good deal of its humor to *Krazy Kat*. The bricks, mesas, and open horizons of George Herriman's work are clearly visible in the Klan paintings of the late 1960s and reappear, though at increasingly distant intervals, during the 1970s. Guston also emulated the shape-shifting that goes on at the peripheries of Herriman's frames. Nevertheless, the peculiar comedy of *Krazy Kat* was more important for Guston. He adopted Herriman's method of depicting a series of variations on a limited set of themes and an equally limited dramatis personae who move about in a blasted abstract landscape. As David Carrier has noted about Herriman's strip, the action of *Krazy Kat* rests on an apparently endless repetition of a small circuit of sublimated desire and aggression. Ignaz throws a brick at Krazy; Krazy adores Ignaz and interprets the missiles as affection; Offisa Pup tries to protect his beloved Krazy by locking little Ignaz in jail. And so it goes, in an infinite round. There is no development and no progress.

Carrier understands this never-ending loop as a form of utopia because it represents freedom from history and change.[46] But one could just as easily claim that *Krazy Kat* depicts a dystopia of repetition and frustration. Herriman was able to render this dystopic vision tolerable, if not sweet, by suspending consequence, that is, by making sure that no action leads to irrevocable results. Guston suspended that suspension and returned from Herriman's timeless and thus invulnerable world to our changeable, time-bound realm. He easily transformed the comedy of *Krazy Kat* into the lively melodramas of his own later works.

That said, it would be a mistake to limit discussion of Guston's paintings of the 1970s to the guilt of thoughtlessness or to the spirit's apparently losing battle with the body. A great deal of the commanding pathos of the later work stems from its sensitivity to individual vulnerability and suffering. As Guston's paintings moved from depicting banal evil to illness, incapacity, and flood, natural forces became the agents of violence. In 1975 and 1976 Guston painted a series of floods—the triptych *Red Sea* (1975), *The Swell* (1975), and *Blue Light* (1975), as well as *Deluge II* (1975), *Source* (1976), and *Wharf* (1976)—which described general and catastrophic inundation. The triptych describes a pun, for it derives from the foreground of Bernardino Luini's painting of the drowning of Pharoah's host in the Red Sea.[47] Guston rendered the water cadmium red and pink, thus making the Red Sea quite literally red. He got rid of the martial motifs of the original. No horses and no wagons appear in his version and certainly no armor. Instead of those wagons he depicted the back of stretchers on the bottom right of *Blue Light*. He kept Luini's upturned faces and his own trademark inverted legs, which he found—however fortuitously—in his precursor's painting. Most important, in the end, however, is that by concentrating on the color of the sea Guston omitted the dry land on which the children of Israel safely stand. He thus voided the painting's promise of redemption. By literalizing the sea, he secularized the painting, and by eliminating the promise of redemption, he universalized its disaster. He turned a localized miracle into a catastrophe as general as Noah's flood. And there isn't an ark in sight.

The apparently grim universality of the triptych was quite literally domesticated in *Source* and *Wharf.* The waters in these paintings do not roil as much as rise. In *Source* they threaten to engulf the haloed head of a woman whose hair is braided in a Byzantine coif. Associated in Guston's works with his wife, Musa, this head also appears in *Wharf.* Ross Feld claimed that Guston lent the figure "something even a little trashy and sentimental." She is, Feld maintained, "the Sphinx, but with a Joan Crawford-ish martyred look."[48] Perhaps the upturned eyes of this figure do not—or, rather, do not merely—signal her melodramatic sense of martyrdom, as she stands next to the figure of a painter whose look is ambiguously trained on both the canvas in front of him and the array of legs to his left. Like her iconographic forebears, she can be taken to be gazing toward heaven, or it could well be that she is gazing up because the waters have reached the level of her eyes. There is no wharf in the painting.

This sense of domestic fragility is underscored in the paintings that were occasioned by Musa's stroke in 1977—*Head* (1977) and *Tears* (1977)—and then continued in *Couple in Bed* (1977), *Sleeping* (1977), and *Night* (1977). In *Sleeping*, which is perhaps the least catastrophic of the paintings of this period, a foreshortened male body pulls red covers up around its head as it lies in a bed that is canted upward against the picture plane. This foreshortening makes the head very large in comparison to the body, with its skinny hairy legs, red pajamas, and big pink shoes. The disproportion between the size of the head and the body, surprisingly feminine eyelashes, and the hand's grip on the bedclothes make this clearly balding man look like a sleeping baby and thus lend the figure its sense of great vulnerability.[49]

The sentimentality that Feld noted in the late works can be located in the exposed isolation of Guston's figures, but to concentrate unduly on this pathos is to miss the corrosive wit that enlivened Guston's paintings in the second half of the seventies. If the forces of nature (and age) took on the threatening agency of the Hoods, a peculiar antic animation brought to life what had previously been the inert lumber of Guston's earlier canvases. A huge pile of shoes has commandeered the composition of *The Door* (1976). The shoes appear to have burst through the door of room 660, and they fill the door frame almost to the top. There are no human or humanoid figures in the work, just a whip on the left-hand wall, clock on the right, lightbulb in the center, and brushes on the floor. In other words, the picture really is a still life in that it has caught all this stuff in motion. In *Monument* (1976) naked legs wearing shoes pile up in the center of the canvas, each trying to move in a different direction. They wriggle around in an abstract, perhaps public, space, but they form an odd monument, because they are hardly stationary or statuesque. The odd humor of this monument becomes even clearer in *Feet on Rug* (1978), in which two feet, with their legs apparently severed in mid-calf, stand on a small fringed red rug, which in turn stands adrift in a sumptuously painted but empty exterior space. Abstracted from their homely indoor habitat, these bare feet are both incongruous and peculiarly dignified—an uncanny monument to the unknown foyer.

One of the traditional definitions of the uncanny locates it at that point where the inanimate becomes animated, where the boundary between the living and the dead, the human and the inhuman, gets fudged. In Guston's later works the dead *disjecta membra* of the paintings of the period from 1968 through 1972 were summoned to life, or the limbs and instruments of even earlier paintings were given a life of their own. In *The Street* (1977) legs in battle formation march against arms with trash can lids in a war of arms against legs. The situation is taken from Guston's earlier work *Martial Memory* (1941), but the composition has nothing of the staged static quality of its precursor. Whereas *Martial Memory* presented the mock warfare of children, the massed limbs of *The Street* are clearly those of adults, and there is no indication that they are indulging in play. What makes the later painting both funny and somewhat eerie is that there are no bodies in the picture, although there is a hint (the trash barrel on the right) that the arms might be attached to something. The legs, though, are left on their own.

In *Entrance* (1979) the disembodied legs mass from two directions (through the door on the left and from the edge of the canvas on the right), the soles of their feet raised against the lovingly painted and rather gentle-looking bugs that are coming through the door. Whether those bugs are victims or invaders, cotenants or intruders, is not clear. In the stark apocalyptic paintings of 1979, the bugs got the upper hand. In *Ravine* (1979), which bears no trace of human presence, the bugs inherit the earth. In *Moon* (1979) they have become enormous. In these last paintings, however, the bugs do not serve the same function as the floodwaters of 1975 and 1976. They do not bear the human away. They take over once the human has disappeared.

In a 1976 review Thomas Hess celebrated Guston's "celestial stupidity," his "willingness to make 'dumb' shapes, inexpressive lumps, ugly or repellent blobs." Hess went on to call this tendency of Guston's "a kind of reverse Pop Art—instead of banal subject matter, he exploits banal pictorial units."[50] True, Guston had no problem with resorting to truly old-fashioned compositional techniques and filled his hierarchical compositions with banal lumps and blobs. But he did not stop with this formal banality, which, as Pincus-Witten had noted in 1970, was quickened by Guston's gorgeous handling of paint and his raucous sense of humor. Guston was also fascinated by the most banal of objects. As he worked through the 1970s, Guston moved from the banality of evil to an uncanny recuperation of what is normally understood as banal—refuse and junk. Guston's late works therefore do represent a reverse form of Pop art. Where Tom Wesselman, Andy Warhol, and James Rosenquist played off the glamour of the commodity, Guston showed what happens when all that glamour has been stripped away. Once goods and people have lost their star power, they become clutter. But their vulnerability lends pathos to their predicament. They might be ridiculous, but they are not necessarily contemptible.

In Guston's paintings after 1974 human violence and the laws of nature became indistinguishable. We could even say that human violence was transformed into a sheer force of nature. These late works figure alienated nature as a form of brute physicality, a massy literalness. As his works moved from the Hoods of the Marlborough show to the insects of *Ravine* and *Moon*, they became increasingly less concerned with analysis. They surrendered themselves to a vision of amused horror. They no longer sought out the source of that horror—the banal violence of thoughtlessness—but concentrated on what it left in its wake: the individual body, suffering from desire, deterioration, and the threat of complete annihilation.

THREE

Allegory

Wherever Guston lived, he hung three reproductions in his kitchen: Piero della Francesca's *Flagellation*, Paolo Uccello's *Battle of San Romano*, and Albrecht Dürer's *Melencolia I*. At first blush these works have little to do with one another, but Dore Ashton quotes a letter in which Guston proposes an odd reciprocal interpretation in which Piero, like Dürer, becomes something of an allegorist.[1] As early as 1972 Guston described his own works as allegories, although he did not discuss exactly what he meant by allegory until 1977.[2] At a public conversation in Boston that year, he acknowledged that he was attracted to allegory precisely because it seemed so unmodern.

As I have shown, Guston's rejection of high modernist vanguardism only added to his cachet by the late seventies, and he was generally respected (and in some circles celebrated) by the time of his death in 1980. But the moment of his final acceptance coincided with the quick rise of postmodernism, which then eclipsed Guston's reputation. Because his concerns were ultimately not those of the postmodernist critics, they were not interested in him. Yet their lack of interest shows us more or less precisely what Guston was doing, because their distance is most clearly visible at precisely the place where their concerns seem closest—in the theory of allegory.

In Boston in 1977 Guston cited *Pit* (1976) as a good example of his allegorical work.[3] *Pit* is one of his series of apocalyptic paintings from 1975 and 1976, a group that includes *Deluge II, Wharf, Red Sea,* and *Blue Light* (see discussion in chapter 2). Whereas these other works depict devastation by flood, *Pit* describes destruction by fire. Robert Storr refers to its "morbid jumble of legs" that have been cast into a pit, its rocky landscape, and its blood-red rain to "images of the Last Judgment . . . where the hierarchic levels of the universe are arranged in balcony-like tiers."[4] While the painting might draw on Renaissance notions of cosmic justice, it is hard to see any particular justice in Guston's painting. It makes no reference to salvation and shows no angels hovering in the empyrean. Guston's symmetrical twin fires give us a particularly Earth-bound vision. Heaven exists merely as a direction (up) and as the apparent source of the deluge. A ladder, borrowed from Dürer's *Melencolia I* as well as from Bill Holman's comic *Smokey Stover,* does not offer a way out of the pit, because all the legs in the painting have been planted upside down and so are forced to sprout like trees. Like *Deluge II,* which shows the brush that is painting the work, *Pit,* with its strange painting within a painting (a ghostly canvas of red rain behind the lip of a pit), emphasizes that it is a work of human hands.

Pit was not the only allegory among Guston's works at the time. His painting *Allegory* (1975) summarizes his motifs of the period— whips, heads, paintbrushes, and disembodied pointing hands.

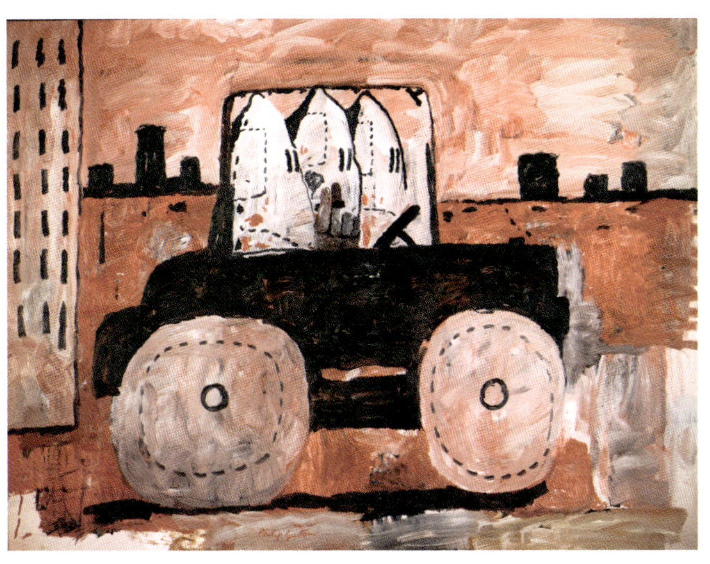

PLATE 1   *City Limits,* 1969. Oil on canvas, 77 × 103¼ in. The
Museum of Modern Art, New York. © The Estate of Philip Guston;
courtesy McKee Gallery, New York.

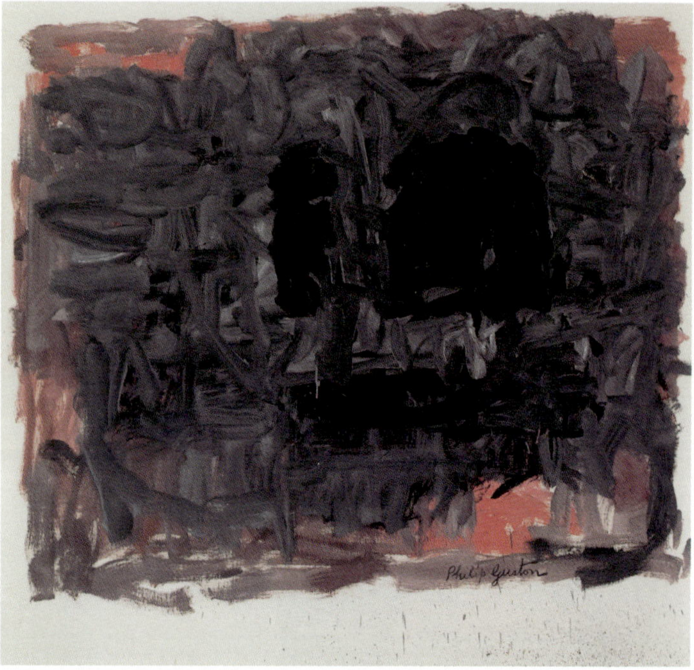

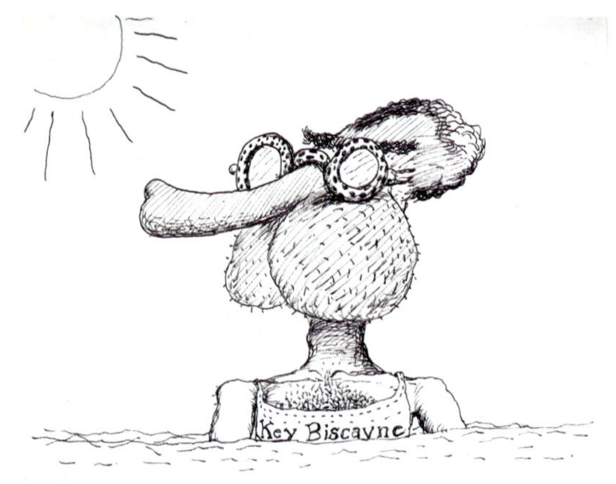

Key Biscayne

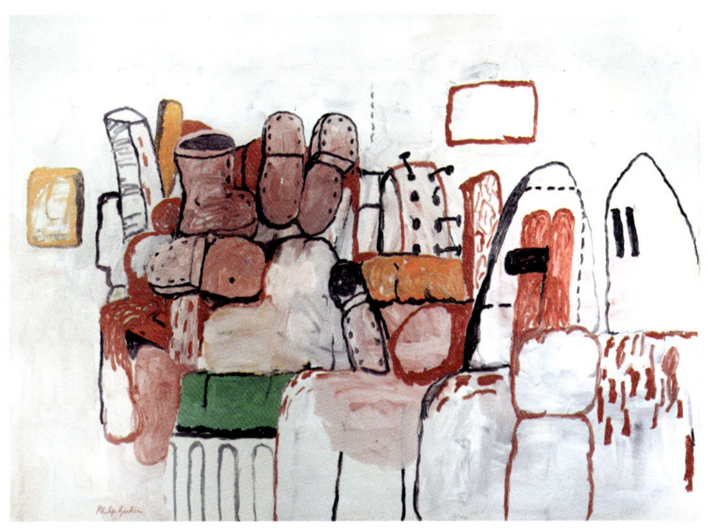

PLATE 2   *New Place*, 1964. Oil on canvas, 75¾ × 80¼ in. San Francisco Museum of Modern Art, Gift of the Artist. © The Estate of Philip Guston; courtesy McKee Gallery, New York.

PLATE 3   *Poor Richard*, 1971. Ink on paper, 10½ × 13⅞ in. Private collection. © The Estate of Philip Guston; courtesy McKee Gallery, New York.

PLATE 4 *A Day's Work*, 1970. Oil on canvas, 78 × 110 in. The Museum of Modern Art, New York, Gift of Edward R. Broida. © The Estate of Philip Guston; courtesy McKee Gallery, New York.

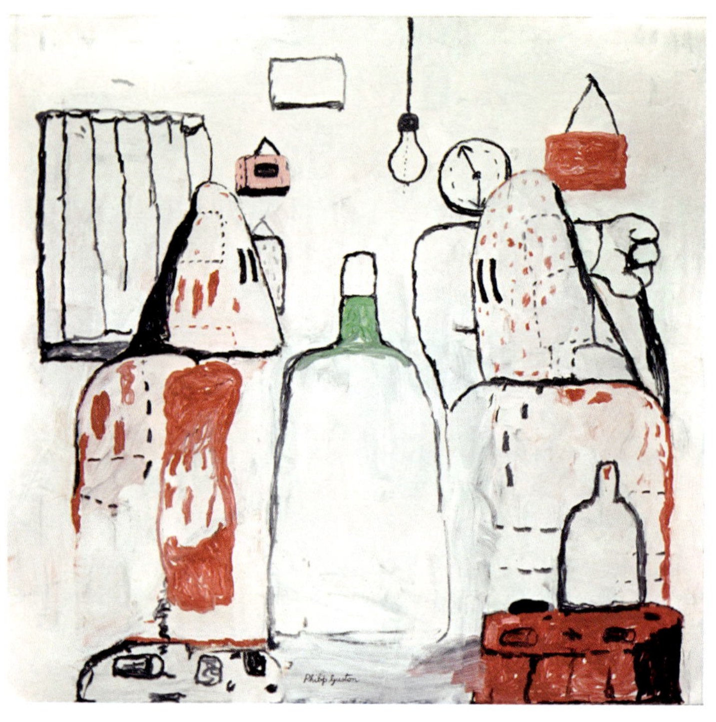

PLATE 5 *Bad Habits*, 1970. Oil on canvas, 73 × 78 in. National Gallery of Australia, Canberra. © The Estate of Philip Guston; courtesy McKee Gallery, New York.

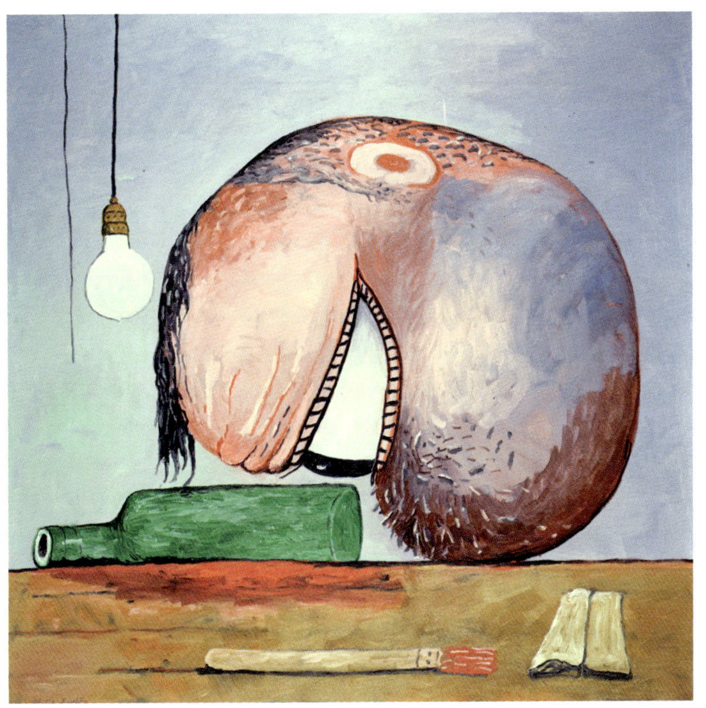

PLATE 6 *Head and Bottle*, 1975. Oil on canvas, 65½ × 68½ in. Private collection. © The Estate of Philip Guston; courtesy McKee Gallery, New York..

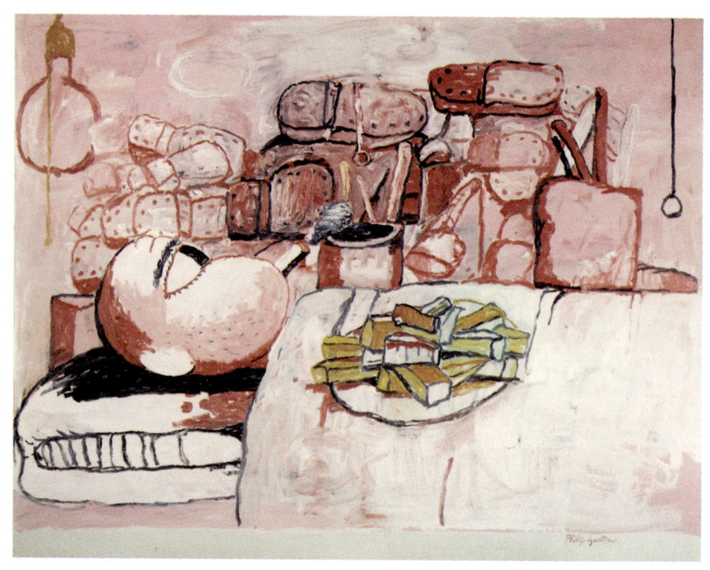

PLATE 7   *Painting, Smoking, Eating,* 1973. Oil on canvas, 77½ × 103½ in. Stedelijk Museum, Amsterdam. © The Estate of Philip Guston; courtesy McKee Gallery, New York.

PLATE 8   Philip Guston and Clark Coolidge, *Signs Put Up on a Boundless Space,* 1972. Ink on paper, 19 × 25 in. Private collection. © The Estate of Philip Guston; courtesy McKee Gallery, New York.

PLATE 9   Philip Guston and Clark Coolidge, . . . *The Space Between Things,* 1972. Ink on paper, 19 × 25 in. Private collection. © The Estate of Philip Guston; courtesy McKee Gallery, New York.

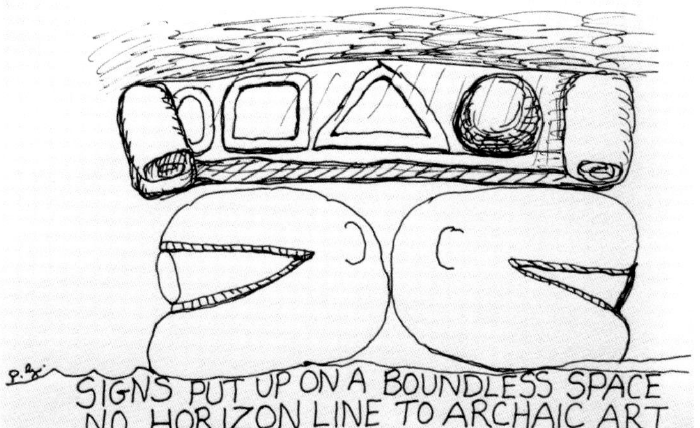
SIGNS PUT UP ON A BOUNDLESS SPACE
NO HORIZON LINE TO ARCHAIC ART...
CLARK COOLIDGE

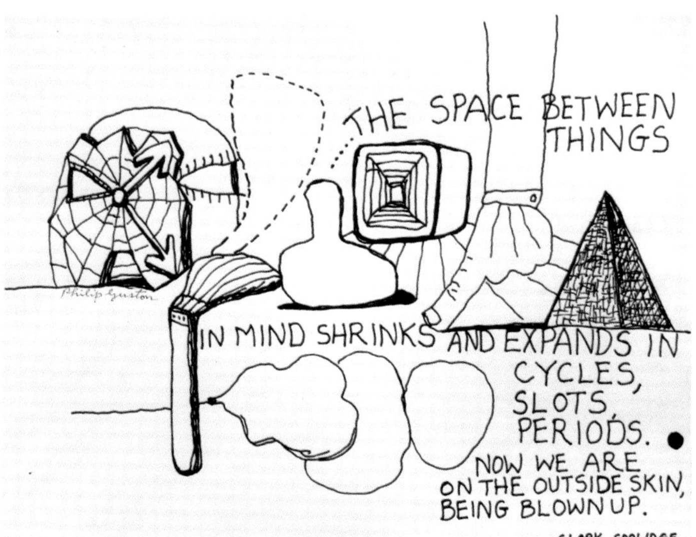
THE SPACE BETWEEN THINGS
Philip Guston
IN MIND SHRINKS AND EXPANDS IN CYCLES, SLOTS PERIODS.
NOW WE ARE ON THE OUTSIDE SKIN, BEING BLOWN UP.
CLARK COOLIDGE

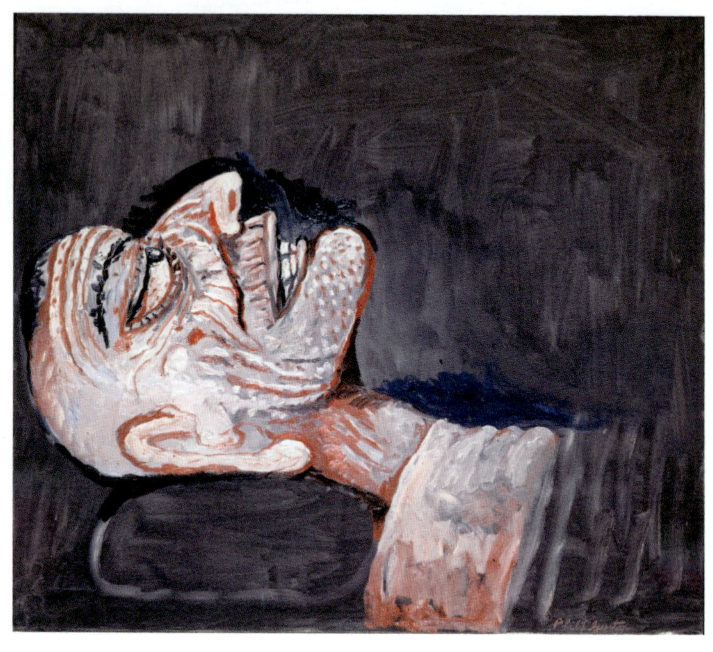

PLATE 10 *East Coker—T.S.E.*, 1979. Oil on canvas, 42 × 48 in. The Museum of Modern Art, New York, Bequest of Musa Guston. © The Estate of Philip Guston; courtesy McKee Gallery, New York.

At the left side of this canvas are a series of emblems—a sphere, square, triangle, and two rulers—all of which Guston has lifted directly from Dürer. The painting's clearly legible words ("The Dilemma: Composer, Painter, Sculptor, Poet") suggest that we *read* these motifs as meaningful signs arranged like a rebus. *Allegory* invites us to decipher the work as a piece of writing, yet that writing is deeply enigmatic. It is as if Guston were interpreting Dürer's *Melencolia I* as a pendant to Giorgio de Chirico's *Jewish Angel*.[5] *Allegory* is self-evidently allegorical. But Guston's decision to call attention to *Pit* as an allegory goes further. It invites us to look for allegory in all the paintings of the seventies.

Guston was not working from what we could call the familiar notion of allegory. The word *allegory* usually refers to a composition made of images or personifications that are all reducible to a conventional set of meanings. These meanings provide a key to the work: a woman might represent liberty (as in Eugène Delacroix's *Liberty Leading the People*) or a bog might represent the weight of despair (as in John Bunyan's *Pilgrim's Progress*). But *Allegory*'s enigmas are hardly conventional, and its meanings are elusive. The same can be said of *Flatlands* (1970), which was featured in some ads for the Marlborough exhibition. In it Guston forces disparate motifs into a foreshortened, crowded space that cannot be read as natural, because each object seems to imply its own perspective. It is a purely semiotic space—like a sentence—shared by the standard lumber from the Marlborough paintings. A range of associations allows viewers to read the painting in divergent ways, depending on which motifs they choose to emphasize. If the Hoods stand in relation to the legs in the front and the chimney in the back, they can be taken as ciphers of the Holocaust. But that interpretation does not account for the painting's books, hand, or rising sun. *Flatlands* does not appear refer to a stable preexisting matrix of signs. Taking it as an allegory requires paying attention to its profuse lack of unity, the relative independence of its objects, and their associative juxtaposition.

We know from Ross Feld that Guston's decision in 1977 to publicly call his recent body of work allegorical was influenced by his reading of Charles Rosen's review of Walter Benjamin's *Origin of German Tragic Drama* (*Tauerspiel*—literally, "mourning play"), which was published that year.[6] Guston, like most postmodern critics indebted to Benjamin, did not actually have a chance to read the book. Its American publication was tied up for several years by a copyright dispute. Guston's interpretation depended on Rosen's.[7] We know from Ross Feld that Guston was fascinated by the idea that the work of art is subject to time and ruin, a notion that serves as the fulcrum of Benjamin's antiorganic aesthetic of fragmentation. In his study of the German *Trauerspiel,* Benjamin reverses the Romantic glorification of the organic symbol over the inorganic script of allegory. According to Benjamin, Baroque allegory presents itself as a mode of writing that cannot be comprehended instantaneously. It must be pondered and deciphered piece by piece. Allegory therefore rejects unity and insists on internal disjunctions: "It is as something incomplete and imperfect that the objects stare out from the allegorical structure."[8]

Allegory delivers a negative judgment on the sublunary world. Allegorical technique presents life as an illusion that, when dissipated, has no substance behind it. Seventeenth-century allegory stresses "discontinuity, an irresolvable discrepancy between a visual sign or image and its meaning."[9] The idea that the world is nothing more than a dream was hardly peculiar to seventeenth-century Germany. But German allegories of that period get their particular pathos from the further conviction that stripping away the illusion does *not* reveal the truth. There is no direct passage from the language of men to the tongues of angels, from immanence to transcendence. The promises of religion are false. Benjamin argues that post-Reformation theology resulted in an impasse that rendered faith impossible, an impasse at the heart of allegory. In a world that offers no path to heaven, allegory can treat objects only as impenetrable foreign signs, dead words abandoned by a living, but hopelessly distant, spirit.

According to Benjamin, seventeenth-century allegory takes the opacity of language as an indication of a specific metaphysical loss—the historical retreat of revelation. The complexities of Baroque allegory derive from a deep melancholy over that loss of transcendence and, with it, the loss of meaning that revelation promises. On a practical level this means that, although allegory depends on both linguistic and iconic conventions, it refuses a one-to-one translation between them. Instead, it melds word and image into hieroglyphs, which are all the more fascinating because they are so cryptic.

Guston's collaborations with the poet Clark Coolidge are clearly allegorical in Benjamin's sense of the term. In the sixties Coolidge often constructed his experimental poems from disconnected words, phonemes, and morphemes. At the time of his friendship with Guston in the early 1970s, Coolidge had developed a recombinant style in which words seem to join their neighbors to make grammatical sense but do not—not quite:

> Panels stitch and hood the string
> numbers the shoe piles
> eyes bottle and stuff rocks the head
> couched in hand foots the bill numbers

> the clouds board up as a ball suns
> the wheels brick up the paint.[10]

The ambiguity of this list of recurrent motifs in Guston's work stems in part from the lineation, which often makes it hard to determine whether a word is meant to function as a noun or as a verb. The word *numbers* in the second line looks like a verb, but a plural subject requires a verb in the plural. "Panels" cannot "numbers" the shoe piles. But a shoe can—grammatically speaking—pile numbers. Stuff might rock the head. That head can even be couched in a hand, but the stuff cannot rock the head and foot the bill without some conjunction to join what look like two main clauses.

The poem thus lacks connective tissue between clauses and between lines. It is an inventory, without any *ifs*, *ands*, or *buts* to hold it together. In this way Coolidge catches Guston's work at its most atomistic, at the point where the precise relations between isolated motifs are hard to pin down and interpret. In a concise and accurate summary of Guston's compositions, Coolidge writes, "Objects are singles are never single."[11] Guston's drawings returned the favor by translating the abstractions of Coolidge's noun/verbs into visual images of concrete objects. In a particularly telling instance, Guston does real violence to his source text, splitting one of Coolidge's poems into two drawings, misquoting it, and deleting one and a half lines.

These changes, as much as Guston's drawings, serve as commentaries on the writing. Here are Coolidge's first two lines, to which Guston devotes a drawing (plate 8):

> Signs put up in a boundless space.
> No horizon line to archaic art.

Whether we are to read this couplet as an existentialist account of archaic art (i.e., archaic art has no horizon line because it pitches against the infinite) or as a description of all art (i.e., all art pitches signs against the infinite) is not clear. Guston's drawing tends toward the second reading. Guston's two lima bean heads look in opposite directions under an unfolding banner/scroll on which we see basic shapes—circle, square, triangle, sphere. Guston has rewritten Coolidge's original. "Put up *in* a boundless space" becomes "put up *on* a boundless space" (emphases added). This change helps explain why the drawing is so claustrophobic, why the heads seem pinched between the ground and the banner, and why the banner seems wedged between the heads and the lowering sky. The signs are tacked up between the viewer and infinity, not framed by or within infinity, and act as a screen or a shield against the boundlessness of space.

Guston cuts two lines from Coolidge's poem, lines in which the poet deprives infinity of its awe:

> Just as there is no bottom
> line to thought.

There is no horizon line in archaic art just as there is no limit to the profits of thought. The sublime infinity of the mind counters the sublime terror of the infinite as, just as in Kant, the mathematical sublime leads one to realize that one can think beyond infinity. While Coolidge's poem seems to celebrate the incommensurable freedom of the mind, Guston's drawings purposely leave out the traces of consolation. Guston thus omits the saving importance of the mind in Coolidge's poem (plate 9). Without it, the sense of Coolidge's next lines, devoted to the way that objects relate in the mind and not in space, changes:

> The space between
> things in mind shrinks and expands
> in cycles, slots, periods. Now we
> are on the outside skin, being blown up.[12]

In the original poem the growing distance between the objects of thought is a function of the mind's sheer vastness. But the image of the skin blowing up (swelling like a balloon or exploding like a bomb) is unsettling in its grammatical ambiguity. Is the skin being blown up or are we?

Once he has eliminated Coolidge's reassuring vision of thought's heroic capacities, Guston's division of the poem into two drawings makes sense. The second drawing might well be an allegory of the mind, and of the space between objects in thought, but ultimately it falls into incoherence. While the work's pyramid, hand, cube, and bottlelike blob are all linked through the use of perspective, the Janus face to the right—in part a clock and in part a web—stands in an unclear relation to the brush and the other blobs, which look like skins or perhaps balloons. What is more, the spacing turns Coolidge's words into objects. One of the poet's preferred terms in this period is *obduration*, and Guston turns Coolidge's words into obdurate things. They become brute material, unwilling to render up meaning.

Coolidge describes Guston's books as "brick loaves" and asks how they are to be read. In Guston's drawings books are as solid as cuneiform tablets and as illegible as Linear B. There is perhaps no clearer motif of the loss of meaning than a book that cannot be read, though the clarity of the motif makes it a poor example of that loss. In the painting *The Magnet* (1975), an unreadable open book dominates the foreground. A large question mark in the margin of the left-hand page baldly signals its incomprehensibility.

The center of the painting is filled by a lightbulb and chain, a painting of what appears to be a relatively flat seascape in red on a thick stretcher and a round object that at first glance appears to be a compass. It points toward the north (which is always "up") and, like the finger of John the Baptist, toward heaven. But the two numbers (a 2 and the top of a 3) on the face of this compass indicate that the compass can also be read as a clock. We might puzzle out the relation between the unreadable book, red seascape, lightbulb, and compass-clock, but deciphering the painting is less important than pointing out that it is a painting to be deciphered. It turns the viewer's inability to interpret it into its theme. In other words, it is an allegory about allegory, of a piece iconographically, thematically, and compositionally with Guston's other works of the period.

Guston was fascinated by the possibilities of allegory throughout the seventies. His allegorical works from the years before he read Rosen's article can be interpreted in terms of Benjamin's theory of allegory because Guston had studied one of Benjamin's chief sources, Erwin Panofsky's studies of Dürer's *Melencolia I*.[13] Panofsky reads *Melencolia I* as a pendant to *St Jerome in His Study*, as an allegory of a disorderly life lived in competition with the Divine. Melancholy is depicted as an earthly builder. A number of her emblems are taken from the construction trades: the ladder, unfinished tower, and scattered nails.[14] But she is more than just a builder, because Dürer draws on the humanist equation between melancholy and geometry. Melancholics, according to this tradition, have a gift for geometry because their thinking is concrete, not abstract. Geometers tend toward melancholia "because the consciousness of a sphere beyond their reach makes them suffer from a feeling of spiritual confinement and insufficiency."[15]

The pyramids, squares, and spheres so prevalent in Guston's later work thus point to the same spiritual *accedia* as Melancholy's geometric figures in Dürer's print. In their despair melancholics register a historical predicament, the loss of revelation and salvation and thus the loss of meaning. They suffer the victory of pure stuff, the inescapable immanence of the world of things.

Benjamin explicitly aims to diagnose the spiritual crisis that led to the development of Baroque allegory and draws implicit comparisons between sixteenth- and seventeenth-century allegories and the strategies of post-Baudelairean modernism. Benjamin argues that the malaise of immanence that besets the post-Reformation artist besets the modern artist as well. Guston apparently agreed. I have already quoted Guston's lament about the obsolescence of the "known image and symbol" and his sense that their loss "motivates modern painting and poetry at its heart."[16] On another occasion Guston claimed that the modern artist had a particularly difficult task because "today it is impossible to act as if pre-imaging is possible."[17]

The painter and his public do not share a frame of reference, cannot draw on the same semantic resources. Thus the artist does not know what his painting will depict before it is painted, and the audience cannot refer that depiction to a common store of meaning. In many ways Guston is describing his own paintings of the later 1950s and the 1960s, in which accretions of paint create thick forms that seem to lurch into being. By 1965 Warhol had solved this problem by painting the mass-mediated signs and common modern wonders that had taken the place of "pre-images." But, as I have already noted, Guston was not interested in that solution.

The loss of the pre-image traps the modern artist in a world of objects that lack established or immediately comprehensible meanings. As artists construct their images on the fly, the relations between those images and their meaning will be allegorical at best and merely solipsistic at worst. So Guston's constant motif of the bricklike unreadable book acknowledges the modern artist's working conditions. It is an allegory—however facile—of unreadability and an allegory because of its unreadability.

The association of allegory and the unreadable became something of a critical commonplace by the end of the seventies. Paul de Man's book of 1979, *Allegories of Reading* (and the critics' association of deconstruction with Benjamin and allegory),[18] contributed to a flurry of interest in allegory at that time. In 1979 and 1980 *allegory* became, however briefly, a key term in discussions of art. In May 1979 Carter Ratcliff curated the exhibition "Illustration & Allegory" at Brooke Alexander. Joan Simon wrote a fairly long review article on it in *Art in America*. In 1980 *October* published Craig Owens's substantial article, "The Allegorical Impulse: Toward a Theory of Post-Modernism," in two parts, as well as Joel Fineman's "Structure of Allegorical Desire" and Stephen Melville's "Notes on the Reemergence of Allegory." Critical interest in allegory had begun to wane by 1982 when Benjamin Buchloh reappropriated the term for Marxism in "Allegorical Procedures: Appropriation and Montage in Contemporary Art." But what looks like the rapid disappearance of the term from art theory actually signals how well it had been assimilated by 1981. Even though allegory was never explicitly invoked, the arguments its defenders (such as Owens and Buchloh) proposed proved to be central to articles such as Thomas Lawson's "Last

Exit: Painting" in *Artforum* in 1981 and Donald Kuspit's attack on Buchloh in "Flak from the 'Radicals' in 1983. In other words, each side wanted to enlist allegory for its own cause.

This constellation of critics indicates that in the early 1980s the defense of figuration relied on a rehabilitation and a redefinition of *allegory* at the same time that allegory justified different accounts of postmodernism. Guston's work did not figure in any of these discussions, nor was he included in any of the grand postmodernist painting shows of the early 1980s, except for "The New Spirit in Painting" in London in 1981. Why was this? In the first place, Guston was—ironically enough—too old and too established to serve as an example of a "new spirit in painting." More to the point, though, Guston's insistence on the melancholy implications of allegory, on the loss of meaning and transcendence that Benjamin describes, was not ironic. Guston was not interested in photography. And irony and photography were the twin supports of postmodern appropriations of Benjamin.

In 1979 and 1980 Craig Owens defined vanguardist postmodernism as allegorical to its core. He first explored "the eruption of language into the field of visual arts" in a review of Robert Smithson's writings and then expanded it to explain an astonishing array of different practices.[19] In the two-part essay "The Allegorical Impulse: Toward a Theory of Postmodernism" (which appeared in *October* in 1980), Owens argued that almost every movement after Pop was allegorical and therefore postmodern.[20] Owens tried to tie together diverse practices by relating them to the allegorical spirit of the age.[21]

Owens argued that Benjamin was an enemy of theology and metaphysics.[22] He maintained that Benjamin used allegory to eliminate transcendence from art and so did not so much mourn the loss of transcendence as restore writing to its proper dignity. Following this line of reasoning, Owens was able to read Robert Rauschenberg, Robert Longo, Troy Brauntuch, Robert Smithson, Sherrie Levine, and Cindy Sherman as postmodern deconstructors of the transcendent, as true allegorists. These artists all investigated the purely contingent nature of signs and revealed the socially constructed nature of representation.

Owens thus saw allegory as the mode that unites the postmodern canon that Douglas Crimp had already elaborated in his important essay "Pictures." Just as Crimp had celebrated David Salle, Brauntuch, Longo, Levine, and Sherman for uncovering the strata and the social constructions of meaning, so Owens praised them for their clear grasp of the "arbitrariness of sign."[23] Crimp and Owens saw a definite break with postmodernism and all its immediate pasts. Hence their defense of postmodernism assumed a strongly vanguardist accent. It celebrated the new art (and the new institutions) it canonized as revolutionary insurgencies.

Owens's and Crimp's descriptions of the postmodern were clearly persuasive. One finds them reworked in a number of places, most notably in Thomas Lawson's "Last Exit: Painting," published in *Artforum* in 1981, and in Donald Kuspit's "Flak from the 'Radicals'" in 1983.[24] Owens and Crimp also provided a flexible defense. Both Lawson and Kuspit were able to use them to defend those contemporary painterly practices that did not interest Crimp or Owens in the slightest. This flexibility can also be seen in Benjamin Buchloh's 1982 article "Allegorical Procedures: Appropriation and Montage in Contemporary Art." Buchloh also justified vanguard art by claiming it was allegorical and claimed a similar definition of *allegory* for vanguard art. But his avant-garde was different from theirs. By maintaining that the situational aesthetics of the late 1960s and early 1970s constituted "an irreversible change in the cognitive conditions of art" and that a return to the commodified art object would be a form of regression, Buchloh put forward Daniel Buren and Michael Asher as the true vanguardists of the moment.[25]

In the end Owens, Crimp, Lawson, Kuspit, and Buchloh agreed that the purpose of vanguard art is to undo the ideological illusions that surround the institutions of both art and meaning. They all located this undoing in postmodern allegory. They appropriated (a good period term) a deconstructive interpretation of allegory (derived from a very particular reading of Benjamin) in order to validate their preferred artistic practices. In each case they invoked the disjunction between sign and meaning to show how a given artist or a given practice broke with the past through a form of demystifying self-reflection. They described the artist's awareness of the contingency of meaning as politically and socially subversive.

Just as Guston's profile did not match that of the avant-garde of the late 1960s, it did not fit the definition of the vanguard in the early 1980s. Nor did he seem to fit in with the other kinds of art that claimed to stand in the vanguard in the same period but for different reasons. While he might steal from other artists (the late Chirico is one example), he never quoted them ironically. His self-reflections were never giddy or defiant. So even though Guston's work is allegorical in the Benjaminian sense, and even though allegory became a guiding critical principle for a time in New York, Guston's Benjamin was different and therefore so was his sense of allegory.

Visually, this verdict makes perfect sense. Painters like Salle and Longo create allegorical effects by juxtaposing and superimposing motifs in different period styles. The disjunctions occur between surface elements of the work. Guston, on the other hand, maintains a uniform style within a painting. The disjunctions of his work derive from the conflict between the lushness of the painting and the apparent crudity of the drawing.

More important, the mood of the work is very different. The cool ironies of the canonical American postmodernists—Salle, Longo, Levine, Sherman, or Eric Fischl—are miles away from the goofiness, anger, slapstick sentimentality, and existential pathos of Guston's canvases. For Owens, as for the other postmodernist critics, the allegorical display of the sign's inherent arbitrariness is something of a victory, because it leads to an increased understanding of the way the world works. It is the mark of a more rational, less mystified art. In short—and unlike Benjamin—this postmodern notion of allegory is tied, ironically enough, to a progressive notion of history and is pitched against the hope for transcendence. American postmodern allegory does not entail melancholy at all—at least not according to the critics who wrote about it. The postmodernist allegorists wanted to shatter the sign, not try to protect its fragility.[26]

Guston, as it turns out, was a good deal closer to the Benjamin of the *Trauerspiel*. For him the gap between signifier and signified was the result of a grievous historical predicament, the hopeless immersion in a world of sheer immanence. According to Benjamin, the particular situation of seventeenth-century Lutheranism and the doctrine of justification by faith led to a double loss—of the world of human action and objects (rendered meaningless by faith), on the one hand, and the horizon of an impossibly distant transcendence. The modern world, which restricts experience to what can be known and restricts the known to that which can be sensed, involves the modern artist in a similar loss and similar melancholy. The rupture within the sign does not signal the trans-historical essence of language but is a grievous product of a catastrophic history. For the postmodernists the allegorical montage displays the artist's superior knowledge. It embodies an understanding of signification, which is nothing less than cutting edge. For Guston allegory is a form of mourning for an object that has been cast forth into the world without its meaning. Just as Guston's allegories mourn for the suffering individual, they lament the loss of meaning once it has been severed from its embodiments. It is not surprising, then, that Guston's later paintings are so concerned with the subjectivity and the brute thingness of things, for this thingness is precisely the point of their greatest vulnerability and resilience.

There is thus something embarrassing and ungainly about Guston's later works that one does not find even in the most ungainly postmodern works. The canonical American postmodernists were often guilty of what high modernism would call bad taste, but the postmodernists—like the high modernists—were rarely guilty of undue nostalgia. They did not suffer from sentimentality, that is, from unseemly or foreordained affections. The earlier works of Salle, Fischl—even of Julian Schnabel—were saved from sentiment and nostalgia by a kind of knowingness, a hip irony about ways and means that is shared with an insider audience that gets the point. Guston's allegories, in contrast, were melancholic and underwritten by nostalgia, as Lawrence Campbell noted late in 1975.[27] One can sense the nostalgia in Guston's attempt to hark back to old comic strips, to the tenement interiors of the 1930s, to the paintings of his wife after her stroke. In other words, one can trace nostalgia in his later paintings' style, motifs, and subject matter. It shades into overt sentimentality in paintings like *Couple in Bed* (1977) and its pendant, *Sleeping* (1977).

Postmodern critics and theoreticians did not take up Guston's work at a time when allegory was so important because the sincerity of his "bad taste" and his unfulfilled and unfulfillable nostalgia for transcendence rendered the allegorical nature of his later works unrecognizable. They were right to give Guston a pass because his interests and theirs did not coincide. His allegories were marked by melancholy, not postmodern delirium. His sentimentality, really a form of vulgarity, was an inescapable condition, not a game of hide-and-seek with established tastes. If Guston's works were difficult to account for in terms of the teetering, but still potent, modernist assumptions that underscored the negative reviews of 1970, they were equally difficult to respond to in terms of the burgeoning postmodernist assumptions of 1980. His return to favor between 1974 and 1979 took place in the interregnum between the decline of avant-gardist energies during the period of "post-Movement" art and the resuscitation of those energies with the "neo" movements at the beginning of the 1980s.

Such an interpretation of Guston is possible because the vanguardist frisson of American postmodernism has become a matter for historical investigation, and the tonic, if somewhat paranoid, exhilaration that accompanied the disjunction of the signifier from the signified has dissipated. In other words, because we no longer live under the sway of certain modernist or postmodernist assumptions, Guston's rejection of modernist formal unities and his refusal of postmodernist ironies means that his interests and intentions can be approached as something more than mere pathologies or regressions. They can be taken seriously because the postmodern critique of canonical and exclusionary histories of modernism has made us much more aware of the countercanons of modern art that Guston drew on. But to tie Guston to an alternative modernism (or postmodernism) is not enough. His anti-vanguardist solicitation of the audience, interest in banality, and insistence on what can be called either sentimentality or nostalgia are all related to Guston's star turn as a Jewish comedian.

FOUR

Jewish Jokes

After a serious heart attack in 1979, Guston painted *East Coker—T.S.E.* (plate 10). He started it as a self-portrait, but he found rather quickly that he was working on a picture of T. S. Eliot.[1] Although Guston admired Eliot and professed affection for his poem "East Coker," the painting remains alarming. In fact, its first owner returned the work to the gallery in short order, explaining that his wife could not bear to live with it. It is hard to fault her reaction. Guston had expunged all traces of Eliot's bleak hope from *East Coker—T.S.E.* Its strength derives in no small part from its unflinching literalness and its rigorous depiction of carnality. Its strength also derives from its singular refusal of glamour. Nothing is reassuring or particularly heroic about this deathbed shot of the great man.

Dore Ashton's description of the painting tries to restore some existential pathos, if not heroism, to *East Coker—T.S.E.* "Eliot's head," she writes, "on its stony ellipse of a pillow is a keenly alive but dying head." She notes that Eliot's "eyes are widened, looking upward, and the mind is at work but terribly aware of the failing light."[2] By concentrating on the eyes, Ashton omits perhaps the most disconcerting feature of the painting: the bared teeth and upturned lips. Eliot's smile—if indeed it is a smile—is remarkably unpleasant. It is hard to tell whether it is touched with sadism or sarcasm or whether the rictus grin is the involuntary effect of death.

Is Guston's Eliot gazing heavenward, as Ashton indicates? He might well be, but the painting does not indicate that heaven waits for Mr. Eliot. Whatever light shines in the work originates in the figure. Above is nothing but darkness. It is not clear whether the figure's attentiveness signals the promise of redemption or, failing that, at least the humility of the restrained Christian faith that Eliot expresses in the poem:

> Wait without thought, for you are not ready for thought:
> So the darkness shall be the light, and the stillness the
> dancing.[3]

The paradoxes of that last line promise a thought beyond thought and a hope beyond human hope or understanding. It is a hope that transcends the appearances of this time-bound and decay-ridden world. This hint of redemption underwrites the way the last line of the poem ("In my end is my beginning") inverts the poem's beginning ("In my beginning is my end"). That first line is presented as a rather grim reminder of the finality of death and leads to cadences that draw from the burial service in the Book of Common Prayer ("Old fires to ashes, and ashes to the earth / Which is already flesh, fur and faeces"). The last line, however, indicates that death is not an end, an absolute boundary, but an incentive to further exploration, to "a deeper communion / Through the dark, cold and empty desolation." The resolute ugliness of the painting—the livid pink flesh, deep red wrinkles, green background—undermines the poem's attempt at spiritualization. There is no jump into transcendence here, not even a dialectical flip. Guston's Eliot remains in the realm of flesh, fur, and faeces.

This carnal literalism presents the problem of how one is supposed to understand the palimpsest the painting describes, where self-portrait yields to the likeness—however caricatural—of the great modernist poet. What kind of equation is Guston pointing to, and what kind of identification is at work here? As I have shown, the figurative works Guston produced after 1968 were often marked by shape-shifting and visual puns. So Guston has changed into Eliot. In many fundamental ways, though, Guston and Eliot could not be more different, and this difference is precisely what gives *East Coker—T.S.E.* its edge. Eliot's insistence on the question of origins in "East Coker" is not merely metaphysical. It is also biographical. The Eliot family lived in the town of East Coker before emigrating to the American colonies in the 1660s, and Eliot's remains were in turn buried there after his death in 1965. The poet's meditation on the history of houses—dynasties as well as buildings—is, for all its abstraction, thus quite personal. Its Anglo-Catholic tones can be seen as an act of claiming kin and claiming WASP legitimacy (in case there had been any doubt) at the same time. Eliot demonstrates that he comes by the authority of his High Anglican idiom quite honestly. It is natural to him.

Philip Guston, on the other hand, was born Phillip Goldstein. His parents were Jews from Odessa who fled during the great upheavals of 1905. After a stop in Montreal, where Phillip was born, they ended up in Los Angeles. Guston's father had a hard time finding work in Southern California and wound up making his living as a junk man before committing suicide in 1923 or 1924. Guston, who never formally graduated from high school, changed his name in 1935, apparently out of a desire to impress his future in-laws.[4] Guston later came to regret this move, and Feld noted that in later life Guston was very clear about his identity: "With Yiddish habitually and liberally thrown into his speech, he had no problem seeing as well as presenting himself as a doubt-ridden" Jewish painter.[5]

If, as Eliot says, "Home is where one starts from," the doubt-ridden Jewish painter thus stood far from the doubt-ridden Anglican poet. It is hard to imagine that the terms in which their doubts are expressed could be mapped onto each other with any ease. This dis-ease is bodied forth in Guston's resolutely carnal painting. Guston could not assume, or even allow Eliot to assume, the ghostly humility of "East Coker." To Guston, Eliot's patient unknowing looked suspiciously like self-satisfaction. And to the doubting Jew the temporal dissolution that is eternity itself dissolved back into time. Guston's Eliot peers into an endless future. The painting therefore serves as a critique of Eliot and his poem. What is more, it serves as an act of negative self-definition for the painter. Guston was not like Eliot. This refusal of identification gives the painting its rather brutal power.

A famous story—most likely apocryphal—is told about Sidney Morgenbesser, the late philosopher at Columbia University. (It is also recounted about others. I first came across it as a tale about Saul Kripke.) It seems that at a professional lecture a noted scholar announced that while a double negative is known to mean a negative in some languages and a positive in others, no natural language had yet been discovered in which a double positive means a negative. From the back of the room Morgenbesser is said to have piped up, "Yeah, yeah." He thus demolished the speaker's argument with a colloquial Yiddishism. One can imagine Guston's *East Coker—T.S.E.* as a similar answer to the Christian hope of Eliot's poem—an agreement and an identification that serve as a negation. Yeah, yeah, indeed.

Guston was not like his friend Mark Rothko or like Barnett Newman, both of whom approached the question of their Judaism in different ways. Rothko is particularly interesting because he was close to Guston and because Rothko's ambivalence toward Judaism was so evident. He changed his name from Rothkowitz. He said, somewhat belligerently, that "he'd never do a synagogue, if he did anything it would be for a Catholic church."[6] And, of course, Rothko did go on to paint the de Menil chapel in Houston. Yet Rothko always defined himself, and not without pride, as a Jew. Stanley Kunitz, who knew him well, described him as "the last rabbi of western art."[7]

In her monograph on Rothko, Dore Ashton stutters when she approaches the paradox of the painter's identity. She speculates that the chapel presented "an opportunity to stand back and generalize his deepest feelings about existence."[8] But there is no reason why Rothko could not have generalized his deepest feeling about existence in a synagogue. Ashton is really pointing to something else—the charge of sectarianism—which would stick to Rothko had he painted a synagogue. The need to "generalize," to paint in an idiom that would not be alienating in its particularity, was evidently the price of being taken seriously as a painter.

For Rothko this demand that he express the universal meant a form of constant code shifting that played out on a number of different levels. Robert Motherwell remembered that "the highest praise in Rothko's vocabulary . . . was to call someone a 'human being.'" Ashton defines that as "a person who feels."[9] I suspect that something important has been lost in the translation here. "Human being" is, of course, the literal rendering of the Yiddish mensch, which conveys more than an empathic soul. It connotes steadfastness and decency. Rothko used the English term and risked misunderstanding because of it.

James Breslin asserted that Rothko "wished to be thought of as a religious but not as a specifically Jewish painter," as if there were such a thing as a religion without institutions or traditions, as if one could just be religious without subscribing to any particular beliefs.[10] While Rothko's desire betrayed a certain willful naïveté, it reflected the reality of the art world in the 1950s. Had he been an overtly Jewish painter, he would have been banishing himself to the margins. Rothko's work thus represented a compromise that of necessity entailed the creation of beautiful infinities without any content. Ashton again gets it both right and wrong when she writes that "Rothko sought a godless expression of godliness."[11] Rothko was faced with the problem of depicting the godly in terms that everyone could accept. Thus he was forced to use terms that lacked all specificity. His work was hardly godless, even in its despair. It just could not address God by any Hebrew names.

Rothko's solution to his Jewish question—avoiding overtly Jewish references—was largely typical of his generation.[12] Newman, of course, presented a very different profile. If Rothko tried to paint a Jewish God without Judaism, Newman tried to paint Judaism without God. His identification as a Jew was never in doubt. The titles of a number of his paintings were lifted from or referred to Jewish texts. You could make a convincing case that

Newman's interest in the sublime in the forties finally found a home at the end of the decade in the mythos of Judaism, which Hegel called (however disparagingly) the religion of sublimity.[13] Newman, the only native-born New Yorker among the first-tier Abstract Expressionists, never flinched from a good fight. So his ambiguous reaction to the crypto-anti-Semitism of Hubert Crehan's negative review of the French & Company show in 1959 is of some importance, if only to demonstrate just what Newman was up against.

Crehan's attack ended with a complicated bit of play:

> It is a proud and inflexible archaic, male sensibility that Newman expresses, lifted from the Old Testament. But we live in another world, really, one certainly that is in need of the phallic charge, although the new man, I imagine, will be aware that we should have more music with the dancing.[14]

In a sensitive account of this episode, Michael Leja has described Newman's subsequent rebuttal as "a hysterically virile defense against charges of hypermasculinity."[15] Leja argues that Newman was misunderstood during the 1950s because, while he tended to frame all conflict in terms of an opposition between potency and castration, the critics of Abstract Expressionism interpreted all conflict as a battle pitched between the masculine and the feminine.[16] Where Newman saw a struggle against weakness, the critics imagined a fight between the genders. This lack of congruence in their concerns meant that Newman never received the interpretations he felt he deserved.

Even though Leja correctly stresses Crehan's attack on Newman's "excessive" masculinity, Leja misses the Pauline thrust that underwrites Crehan's attack. Crehan plays off Paul's distinction between the old law and the new and is therefore able to pun on the artist's name in drawing the equally Pauline distinction between the outmoded man of the Old Testament and the new man born in Christ. If we pay attention to the supersessionist rhetoric of Crehan's quip, we can see that he is clearly claiming that Newman, a "stiff-necked and obdurate" (Crehan calls him "proud and inflexible") child of the old order, has no place in the new dispensation. Newman's hyperbolic masculinity would seem to be of a piece with his adherence to the wrathful God of the Old Testament. A symptom of his larger problem is his embarrassing identification with an archaic faith.

In his classic, though now generally ignored, study of Jewish assimilation, John Murray Cuddihy anatomizes the kind of bias that shaped Crehan's comments. Cuddihy argues that Jewish emancipation demanded the sacrifice of older manners and the adoption of "the Protestant esthetic and the Protestant etiquette."[17] The path to inclusion in the modern state lay in the adoption of new forms of polite public behavior. The cost of this inclusion was "the bifurcation of private affect from public demeanor" and the adoption of an inoffensive decorum.[18]

Civility thus requires the banishment of religious particularity and replaces it with a surface ecumenism. This, as Murray notes in a scathing reading of Bernard Malamud and Saul Bellow, turns out to be nothing more than Protestantism in drag. If the notion of Jewish incivility was the subtext for Crehan's attack, Crehan clearly was accusing Newman of being too pushy, of being too much a Jew.

Newman did not respond directly to the Pauline rhetoric or to the anti-Semitic implications of Crehan's review.[19] Instead, as Leja recounts, Newman focused—however hysterically—on the charge of hypermasculinity. While Newman might have been overly sensitive to questions of masculine power, it is also likely that Crehan touched on a dangerous point that Newman felt he could not counter. Newman's Jewish sublimities could have been a little too sublime. They might seem too particular to be generalized. In other words, Newman's images might not achieve the universal self-evidence he desired. They threatened to retreat into the sectarianism of minority religious reference. Majority religious reference is apparently never sectarian, or, as Margaret Olin writes acidly, "Some peoples are more universal than others."[20]

The fear that Newman's work might be construed as "too Jewish " crops up in (of all places) Thomas Hess's catalogue essay for the Museum of Modern Art's posthumous retrospective of Newman's work. Even though Hess went out of his way to argue that the kabbalah provided a master key to Newman's work, Hess also wanted to make it clear that "Newman was not involved in any of the orthodoxies or tribal customs of the Jews." He assured the reader that "no artist is less ethnic" and that Newman was "the American cosmopolitan, mid-twentieth century."[21]

In many ways, of course, Hess was right. Harold Rosenberg noted that Newman's version of Judaism represented "a one-man culture . . . estranged from shared ideas."[22] Newman's understanding of Judaism was deeply idiosyncratic, and he obviously felt that the kabbalah and Genesis provided him with universally valid images of "man's birthright, his urge to be exalted."[23] Nevertheless, Hess's defense of Newman—that the painter did not take part in the (primitive?) "tribal customs of the Jews"—is odd. Hess appears to be saying that it is perfectly all right for Newman to use Jewish references because in the end he did not really believe in them. Hess thus indicated that Newman's lack of faith rendered the work universal. Because Newman's paintings confronted the rupture with tradition, they depicted the pathos of modern man—"alone, surrounded by chaos . . . a transient being—absurd."[24] In other words, Hess defined Newman, not altogether accurately, as a pessimistic existentialist. Hess thus ignored the optimism of the political anarchist who praised Kropotkin's scrupulous "defense of the untrammeled person."[25]

By casting Newman in this role, Hess hoped to render him "civil." So Newman's case ended up resembling Rothko's. The experiences of both painters show that broad acceptance could be purchased only through the ambivalent assertion of a Judaism that was not quite Jewish.[26] Even though Guston said that it was "better to die a Jew than a bohemian," there is no indication that he had any hankering to return to religious practice.[27] Ross Feld wrote that Guston's "left-over leftist iconoclasm certainly included religion." Guston evidently told stories of "Yom Kippur dinners and mock-Seders with the Rothkos that involved shrimp."[28]

Nevertheless, as Feld was the first to note, the rolls of canvas in Guston's later pictures look a lot like Torah scrolls.[29] These scrolls popped up in the paintings of 1975: in the foreground of *Head and Bottle;* propped up against the background of *The Paw II;* lying on the pitched tabletop of *Head and Table.* The ambiguity between canvas and scroll is telling, for the scrolls are either empty or rolled up. Their content is thus hidden. They act as ciphers of a terrible double blockage—unreadability and an inability to paint.

Guston was aware of himself as a Jew who lacked the requisite faith. Rather than follow Newman and treat Jewish themes as universal myths, Guston turned to a literary model, Isaac Babel, the Jewish Soviet writer whom I had occasion to mention in the second chapter. We would do well to follow Guston's lead. Guston once discussed the "lovely, ironic speech" that Babel gave before the Soviet Writers Union in 1934. Babel ended his talk by saying that the Soviet regime had given the writers almost everything but had deprived them of one important privilege, "that of writing badly." Guston went on to ask, "Doesn't anyone want to paint badly?"[30]

Babel had to resort to a kind of code, and "writing badly" could only have meant breaking with the strenuous banality of party-sanctioned "realism." In Guston's context "painting badly" could only mean breaking with Clement Greenberg's ethos of purity and the pieties of a modernist vanguardism. It meant overcoming the reticence that various modernisms maintained in order to avoid acknowledging the uncomfortable fact of "art's actual belonging to the pathos of bourgeois taste."[31] In order to paint "badly," one would have to be willing to forget the long-standing ban on sentimentality, nostalgia, and self-absorption—that is, the ban on kitsch—by which American avant-gardes had tried to distance themselves from the supposedly middle-brow tastes of the bourgeoisie.

If we accept Cuddihy's argument that Jewish emancipation required the adoption of alien rules of decorum, then Guston's identification with Babel and his call to "write badly" becomes more interesting.[32] By rejecting certain modernist decorums, Guston signaled his awareness of the subterranean connection between assimilation and high art.[33] His refusal of decorum served as a way of marking his work as Jewish. In this way Babel could serve as a guide. In the first place, Babel wrote about Odessa, which had been the birthplace of Guston's parents and thus served as a bridge to Guston's own roots.[34] More to the point, Babel's rambunctious humor and sentimental pathos derived from his own ambivalent relation to Judaism.

As I noted in chapter 2, the joke of Babel's *Red Cavalry* stories (and they are bitterly funny) lies in their recounting of the war-experiences of a nearsighted bookish Jew as he rides through the decimated Polish countryside with a regiment of Cossacks, who were traditionally the agents of the czars' violently anti-Semitic policies. Babel's hero wants desperately to be like the Cossacks. He admires their horsemanship and their savage ability to kill without anger, fear, or passion.[35] Conscience-stricken Jew that he is, Babel's narrator cannot bring himself to murder, though he does indicate—in the final lines of the last story—that he has learned how to master a horse.[36] Contradictions drive Babel's work. From the Rabelaisian accounts of Jewish Odessa to the sentimental "End of the Asylum," Babel's stories get their tone, and often their plots, from the ambiguities of Babel's historical commitments. On the one hand, he was driven by a deep idealized nostalgia for a prerevolutionary Jewish Odessa. On the other hand, his stories registered his awareness that life in that lost world entailed nothing less than a set of grotesque constrictions.

A good child of the Jewish Enlightenment, Babel was torn between embracing the radiant future and mourning the immediate past. This allowed him the self-contempt, self-dramatization, sentimentality, monstrosity of detail, and sometimes terrifying coldness that mark his prose. Babel's style is riven by hyperbole and metaphor, sly juxtapositions, and violence edged with humor. One example will have to suffice, although it will hardly give more than a taste of the rich peculiarities of Babel's writing. Toward the end of *The Red Cavalry*, the narrator watches the death of a great rabbi's son, a young man who deserted his family and his past to fight for the Bolsheviks. The narrator gathers the dying man's belongings and inventories them in their wild diversity. They include portraits of both Lenin and Maimonides; Communist leaflets whose margins are "crowded with crooked lines of ancient Hebrew verse," as well as phylacteries and gun cartridges.[37]

Babel's narrator clearly identifies with the rabbi's son ("I was there beside my brother when he breathed his last"), and he is torn by the same contradictions: between Judaism and Bolshevism, religious longing and political propaganda, sensuality and the demands of party discipline. To a certain extent the death of the rabbi's son is absolutely necessary—history cannot reconcile the opposites the young man embodies. These tensions threaten to rip the narrator apart as well. Their violence twists his language into an odd metaphor in which the Bible and cartridges drizzle down in a "sad, sparse rain."

The schematic oppositions of this passage and its melodrama make it "bad" writing and a model for Guston. Guston claimed Babel as kin at least three times in print. In 1970, as I noted in chapter 2, he pointed to Babel's subject matter: "Like Babel with his Cossacks, I feel as if I have been living with the Klan."[38] In 1977 Guston quoted Babel's speech to the Writers Union. And finally, in 1980, he said that he liked Babel because "because he deals totally with fact." Guston maintained that nothing could be more startling than a simple statement of fact in a certain form. And then he quoted Babel, who said that "there is no iron that can enter the heart like a period in the right place."[39]

Guston's stress on fact could be misconstrued as an indication that he looked to Babel for some kind of verisimilitude. But Babel's comment about the period has to do with style and rhythm. Babel did not teach Guston about realism but about the importance of juxtaposition. What is more, Babel was interested in the work's emotional effects. Babel's desire to go straight for the heart moved directly against modernism's proscription of those affective vestiges of mass culture—melodrama and cheap sensation.

One feature of Babel's lack of decorum—his refusal of moderation—is that his prose is haunted (even in translation) by Yiddish.[40] And his insistent lack of decorum, deriving as it does from his thematized ambivalence about the costs of modernization and assimilation, makes Babel sound particularly Jewish, even as he is trying to pattern himself on Guy de Maupassant. In a very real way Babel's stylistic incivility signaled his inability to pass. A more recent example of Babel's refusal can be found in Guston's great friend of the early seventies, Philip Roth.

After the WASP mimicry of *When She Was Good,* Roth clearly jettisoned all decorum and produced his enraged, enraging, and scandalously funny account of the pains of Americanization in *Portnoy's Complaint* (first published in 1969).[41] Like Babel's work, *Portnoy's Complaint* was born of ambivalence. On the one hand, Roth clearly felt a strong nostalgia for the anchors of Jewish identity, and, on the other, he expressed an equally strong desire for full assimilation. The book's manic force derives principally from this tension. Portnoy's rage and Roth's prose are propelled by the delicious irony that the more success Portnoy has with shikses, the more he succeeds with his sexual conquest of sheer Americanness, the more he is defined as a Jew.[42] As Portnoy says, he is living in the middle of a Jewish joke.[43]

Critics commented from the start that *Portnoy's Complaint* is structured like a stand-up monologue about Jewish stereotypes: overbearing phallic Jewish mothers, weak fathers, and guilty sons.

But it is as much the rhythm and the method of the writing that make *Portnoy* read Jewish, make it sound like a *shpritz*—the comedian's torrent of words, spit, and invective. In his biography of Lenny Bruce, Albert Goldman anatomizes a particular New York version of the Jewish comic monologue, though its general features are hardly specific to New York. The *shpritz* was an unholy mixture of seriousness, intellectuality, wild parodies, and paranoid extravaganzas. It was, as Goldman notes, hyperbolic. It was "loud, violent strained and forced." The decorum (the word is Goldman's) of prose "was short-circuited impatiently. Bang, bang, bang!"[44]

The *shpritz* is marked by its exaggeration and its aggression, and this aggression served as the motor force behind the sheer speed of its inventions. *Shpritzing* was specifically Yiddish because it turned the kvetch into a form of art, and it derived, however distantly, from the rabbis' equally aggressive habit of arguing by puns, of proving their intelligence through inspired associations.[45] Nothing could be further from the accepted canons of acceptable logic or good taste. If Bob Newhart signaled his WASP heritage through litotes—the trope of understatement—the *shpritzer* (be it Lenny Bruce or Alex Portnoy) claimed Jewish kin through his use of indecorous hyperbole.[46] And the whole point of the *shpritz* is that it is most decidedly not civil. It highlights troublesome differences. The *shpritz* types the *shpritzer* as a Jew.

It is too easy to get caught in the trap of seeing Portnoy's *shpritz* as fundamentally sexual, when in fact all the dirty words, the improbable and improbably funny sexual episodes, are an important vehicle for scandal. Beyond his themes, beyond his subject matter, Portnoy might want to escape the burden of being a well-mannered Jewish boy, but his vehemence, his exaggerations, his sheer inventiveness defined Roth as an unrepentantly Jewish writer precisely because his prose refused to play nice, to fall into an alien and alienating civility.[47]

We would do well to see Guston's own breaches of vanguardist decorum—his solicitation of the audience, his "philistine" interest in banality, his unironic traces of sentimentality and nostalgia—as Jewish gestures, however abstract they might seem. It would not be inaccurate to claim that Guston's later paintings are the visual version of a *shpritz.* They are not without their aggression, and they revel in their associative inventions. In fact, they consist of precisely those inventions.

But there is more to Jewish humor than the *shpritz.* Guston's mid-1970s critics attributed the dark humor of Guston's later works to Beckett, but it might have been closer to the truth to claim that Guston's later paintings indulge in both the ethos and the pathos of Jewish jokes. They partake of that particular mixture of pragmatic impatience, hair-splitting idealism, grandiosity, sentiment, and self-loathing that one finds in borsht belt standup. "I can't go on, I'll go on" is as much Rodney Dangerfield as it is the adoptive literary son of Joyce.[48]

As early as 1966 Morton Feldman pointed to the particularly Jewish quality of Guston's work when he claimed that Guston was essentially a Renaissance painter who did not study with the masters but "observed it all from the ghetto—in the marshes outside of Venice." Guston took that art into the diaspora with him. Because of that, "Guston's painting is the most peculiar history lesson we have ever had."[49] In Feldman's conceit Guston had been banished several times. Though a native son of the Renaissance, Guston was already marginal. He watched the great rebirth of arts and letters from the original ghetto. The diaspora in which he finds himself now bears the marks of a triple exile: once from the Holy Land, once from Italy, and once in modernity. As a Jew, he could not take a central role in the Renaissance. As a product of the Renaisssance, he was alienated from the art of the twentieth century. If his work presented "the most peculiar history lesson," it must be because his status as an outsider meant that he could not fit any of the established narratives. He showed how art history worked by being forced outside that history.

Feldman's claim, still somewhat cryptic in 1966, makes more sense in light of Guston's later work. It has been my argument that in order to read these paintings, we have to see them in their often negative relations with the New York art world as well as in terms of what could loosely be called the "inner dynamic" of his interests and obsessions. The question of Jewishness was an important one in that art world, and it also played into Guston's own obsessions. While Rothko and Newman both accepted the twin ideals of transcendence and of universality that drove so much of the discussion of Abstract Expressionism, Guston took a different route, one that Cuddihy has described as a cultural form of religious return, a conversion from "the refinement which is vulgarity to the coarseness which connotes the modern 'authenticity.' "[50]

How was Abstract Expressionist refinement really a kind of vulgarity? In a rich reverie at the end of his book on modernism, T. J. Clark argues that the peculiar strength of Abstract Expressionism lay in its vulgar pushiness, in its odd mixture of sheer vehemence and surface delectation. In his view the best Abstract Expressionist works are marked by "ludicrous bigness and lushness and generality."[51] Clark claims that this vulgarity has deep roots in class relations. Abstract Expressionism "is the style of a certain petty bourgeoisie's aspiration to aristocracy, to . . . the aristocrat's claim to individuality." Clark sees a touching absurdity in this. The petty bourgeois can never, by definition, be an aristocrat. Rather, the petty bourgeois cannot help making a hash of the aristocratic airs that he assumes. The vulgarity of the Abstract Expressionist lies in overdoing it, in the parvenu's knack of getting it just wrong by overdoing what is right.

Clark's argument reverses the terms of the standard apologies for Abstraction Expressionism. Clark asks us to see the refinement, heroic self-assertion, and universalism of the New York School as nothing more than a series of gorgeous pretensions. Clark's thesis, based as it is on class, becomes more pointed and more poignant if we factor in the question of ethnicity. The aristocrat, after all, claims both individuality and representative generality. He speaks for himself and for the whole. This odd and ideologically freighted role devolves upon the bourgeoisie in the nineteenth century. If it is absurd after the Second World War for a member of the petty bourgeoisie to take on such airs, how much more absurd it is for a petty bourgeois member of a religious minority to put him- or herself forward as a representative of the universal.[52]

Guston's later works do not give up completely on the desire to depict the universal (we can find its vestiges in his apocalyptic paintings), but they do seem to acknowledge the untenability of the Abstract Expressionist drive toward generality and transcendence. The aging of Abstract Expressionism, an obsolescence that Guston could see in the relative failure of his 1966 Jewish Museum show, seems to have told him just how unconvincing his assault on Parnassus had become. It might well have also informed just how vulgar—in both Clark's and Cuddihy's sense—such assaults really were. So Guston gave up the striver's aspirations to refinement. To say that Guston adopted a willfully "authentic" coarseness of humor, as Cuddihy's argument would seem to demand, is to follow Hilton Kramer and accuse Guston of a despicably calculated naïveté. It would be more accurate to understand Guston's "coarseness" as a refusal of a false refinement, an acceptance of the philistine, not because the philistine is more authentic but because the artist's snobbery is based on a false sense of superiority. Such a view would explain why, when Guston gave up on the fight against the impure, the philistine, and the banal, he did not fall into either a well-tempered prettiness or into that easy middle-class piety that demands that art be either "positive" or edifying. *East Coker—T.S.E.* is certainly neither pretty nor positive. *City Limits* is not edifying.

In the end Feldman might have gone too far when he argued that Guston provides us with "the most peculiar history lesson we have ever had." Guston shows us how overdetermined artists' work actually is, how artists become what they will be within a thick and complex web of implication that is indeed peculiar to their time. Guston's paintings were produced at a moment when the notion of the avant-garde had just begun to lose its legitimizing importance. They displayed the tension between the all-over Abstract Expressionist and traditional post-Renaissance composition. They rejected certain central tenets of modernism that still had pull in New York. They adhered to the artist's ethnic identity when that was difficult, though not impossible, to do and so were indirect about that identity in particular and nonrepeatable ways. Like all powerful art, Guston's paintings derived their energies from the precise nature of their rejections. These rejections make more sense the more they recede into our recent past, and they become clearer because the impulses they fought against have lost their salience, their apparent necessity. It would therefore be impossible to be Guston again, though it will be difficult to avoid the general implications of his idiosyncratic path.

ACKNOWLEDGMENTS

It has taken a decade for *Telling Stories* to arrive in print, and in that time I have accrued many debts.

Peter Stearns, the provost of George Mason University; Jack Censer, dean of the College of Humanities and Social Sciences; and Robert Matz, chair of the English Department, provided generous funding for the publication of this book.

David McKee, who has shown and championed Guston for nearly forty years, has been gracious from the start.

I benefited greatly from conversations with Bill Berkson, Robert Pincus-Witten, James Hyde, and Charles Stuckey. Archie Rand has been the tutelary spirit of this book.

I have been lucky in the helpful comments from a number of readers, particularly Svetlana Alpers, Bill Berkson, Molly Chehak, James Hyde, Ellen Landau, Charles Stuckey, and Ellen Todd. I am also grateful for the sometimes ferocious rigor of my anonymous reviewers at University of California Press.

I am also thankful for the kind patience of my editor, Stephanie Fay, and am grateful to Sue Heinemann, who saw this book and this author through all the stages of publication.

The many drafts of *Telling Stories* were composed in the interstices of what we call, however oddly, my personal life. I wrote it while my wife, Sharon Squassoni, was at work or while my daughters, Zoe and Lucia, were asleep. As a result the book is truly and gratefully dedicated to them.

NOTES

INTRODUCTION

1. Bill Berkson, "The New Gustons," *Art News* 69, no. 6 (October 1970): 44.

2. Philip Guston, letter to Harold Rosenberg, March 4, 1977, Harold Rosenberg Papers, 1923–84, Research Library, accession no. 980048, Getty Research Institute, Los Angeles.

3. Here is Danto:

> What in the end makes the difference between a Brillo box and a work of art consisting of a Brillo Box is a certain theory of art. It is the theory that takes it up into the world of art, and keeps it from collapsing into the real object which it is. . . .
>
> The artworld stands to the real world in something like the relationship in which the City of God stands to the Earthly City.
>
> *Arthur Danto, "The Artworld," in Steven Henry*
> *Madoff, ed.,* Pop Art: A Documentary History
> *(Berkeley: University of California Press, 1997), 276*

4. Arthur Danto, "The Art World Revisited," in *Beyond the Brillo Box* (New York: Farrar Straus Giroux, 1992), 42.

5. See esp. Pierre Bourdieu, "The Field of Cultural Production," in

The Field of Cultural Production (New York: Columbia University Press, 1992), 29–73, and *The Rules of Art,* trans. Susan Emmanuel (Stanford, Calif.: Stanford University Press, 1996), 46–176.

6. See John Frow, *Cultural Studies and Cultural Value* (New York: Oxford University Press, 1995), 16–60.

7. Bourdieu, *Rules of Art,* 37–40, 75–76, 101, 113–20.

CHAPTER 1: SICK OF PURITY

1. Charlotte Lichtblau, "Galleries," *Arts Magazine* 45, no. 2 (November 1970): 58.

2. See Bill Berkson, "The New Gustons," *Art News* 69, no. 6 (October 1970): 45–47, 85.

3. "Guston seems never to have had to fight against the learned habit of conceiving painting-space as essentially Cubist . . . and when the new space approached him through increasing complications of imagery stimulated by Surrealist emphasis on the subconscious, he was able to make it his own in a very personal way. . . . No longer were his dialogues with Chirico and Giovanni di Paolo, but with the more abstract landscapes of Cézanne, with Tiepolo, Turner and not the late Monet. In finding instinctively a closer relation to Impressionism than to Cubism, Guston confirmed an already hierarchical attitude toward form" (Frank O'Hara, "Growth and Guston," *Art Chronicles 1954–1966* [New York: George Braziller, 1975], 136).

4. See Harry Cooper, "Recognizing Guston," in Joanna Weber, ed., *Philip Guston: A New Alphabet* (New Haven, Conn.: Yale University Art Gallery, 2000), 33–35.

5. "The Philadelphia Panel," *It Is* 5 (spring 1960): 38.

6. Philip Guston, "Faith, Hope and Impossibility," *Art News Annual* 31 (1966; pub. 1965): 152–53, reprinted in Henry Hopkins and Ross Feld, *Philip Guston* (San Francisco: San Francisco Museum of Art, 1980), 42.

7. William Berkson, "Dialogue with Philip Guston 11/1/64," *Art and Literature* 7 (1965): 68.

8. Philip Guston, "Piero della Francesca: The Impossibility of Painting," *Art News* 64, no. 3 (May 1965): 38–39.

9. Guston, "Faith, Hope and Impossibility," 42.

10. For pre-imaging see Richard Wollheim, "Minimal Art," in Gregory Battcock, ed., *Minimal Art: A Critical Anthology* (New York: E. P. Dutton, 1968), 398. For its impossibility see Guston, "Faith, Hope and Impossibility," 42.

11. Hopkins and Feld, *Philip Guston*, 41.

12. Berkson, "Dialogue with Philip Guston 11/1/64," 56.

13. Barry Schwabsky, " 'The Real Situation': Philip Guston and Mark Rothko at the End of the Sixties," *Arts* 61, no. 4 (December 1986): 46.

14. He went on: "The compulsion to move forward, or perhaps simply to move on, is shrinking at an alarming rate the capacity for appreciation, in its finer nuance, of older art which has by no means exhausted its resources or completed its statement" (Sam Hunter, introduction to *Philip Guston: Recent Paintings and Drawings* [New York: Jewish Museum, 1966], n.p.).

15. Hunter's strategy is actually quite cunning because his defense of monotony resembles Barbara Rose's brief for Andy Warhol the year before. But Rose was claiming that art was miming the tedium of modern life. See Barbara Rose, "ABC Art," in *Autocritique* (New York: Weidenfeld and Nicholson, 1988), 55–72.

16. Heinrich Wölfflin, *Principles of Art History*, trans. M. D. Hottinger (New York: Dover, 1950), 14.

17. Ibid., 27.

18. Berkson, "New Gustons," 85.

19. Clark Coolidge and Philip Guston, *Baffling Means* (Stockbridge, Mass.: O-blek Editions, 1991), 84.

20. See Denise Hare's photograph of Guston's studio in Dore Ashton, *A Critical Study of Philip Guston* (New York: Viking, 1976), 155.

21. Cooper, "Recognizing Guston," 37.

22. Musa Mayer, *Night Studio: A Memoir of Philip Guston* (New York: Da Capo, 1997), 151.

23. Thomas B. Hess, "The Abstractionist Who Came in from the Cold," *New York Magazine*, December 7, 1974, 102.

24. Dore Ashton, "That Is Not What I Meant at All: Why Philip Guston Is Not Post-Modern," *Arts* 63, no. 3 (November 1988): 28.

25. Meyer Schapiro, "Recent Abstract Painting," *Modern Art* (New York: George Braziller, 1978), 217–18. The essay was originally entitled "The Liberating Quality of Avant-Garde Art." The present title accepts that abstraction soon lost its avant-garde status.

26. "A Conversation between Philip Guston and Joseph Ablow," 29.

27. Mayer, *Night Studio*, 102.

28. Benjamin H. D. Buchloh, "Conceptual Art 1962–1969: From the Aesthetic of Administration to the Critique of Institutions," *October* 55 (winter 1990): 125. See also Caroline Jones, *Machine in the Studio: Constructing the Postwar American Artist* (Chicago: University of Chicago Press, 1996).

29. Brian O'Doherty, "Art vs. Feeling," in *Object and Idea: An Art Critic's Journal, 1961–1967* (New York: Simon and Schuster, 1967), 209. This essay first appeared in February 1964.

30. Mayer, *Night Studio*, 157.

31. Morton Feldman, "For Philip Guston," in *Give My Regards to Eighth Street: Collected Writings of Morton Feldman*, ed. B. H. Friedman (Cambridge, Mass.: Exact Change, 2000), 198.

32. In his finely nuanced discussion of Feldman's reaction to Guston's work, Ross Feld writes, "With each decade since [Guston's] death it becomes clearer that there was a significant cultural crossroads involved in his heresy, that from Guston modern art achieved a late challenge [that] someone like Morton Feldman simply perceived earlier and more painfully than anyone else (Ross Feld, *Guston in Time* [New York: Counterpoint, 2003], 77).

33. Hilton Kramer, "A Mandarin Pretending to be a Stumblebum," *New York Times*, October 25, 1970, B27.

34. Robert Hughes, "Ku Klux Komix," *Time Magazine*, November 9, 1970, 62.

35. Harold Rosenberg, "Liberation from Detachment," *De-Definition of Art* (New York: Macmillan, 1972), 138.

36. Hughes, "Ku Klux Komix," 62.

37. Robert Pincus-Witten, "New York," *Artforum* 9, no. 4 (December 1970): 74–75.

38. "Guston points to his mode of painting, itself, since a disparity exists between the altitude of the facture and the baseness of the humor. Perhaps the low humor hints that the quality of Guston's painting—I mean that stuff about the organic meaning of the way things are painted—is on the verge of faltering as well" (Pincus-Witten, "New York," 75).

39. Caroline A. Jones, *Eyesight Alone* (Chicago: University of Chicago Press, 2005), 348. Annette Michelson noted something of this currency when she wrote that "there is, in fact, a sense in which Kramer, Greenberg, and Rosenberg all begin, by the late '60s, to move much more closely together in the rhetoric of their defenses and rejections" (Annette Michelson, "Contemporary Art and the Plight of the Public: A View from the New York Hilton," *Artforum* 13, no. 1 [September 1974]: 69).

40. Harold Rosenberg, "Everyman a Professional," in *The Tradition of the New* (reprint, New York: McGraw-Hill, 1965), 60–61.

41. Of course, the business end of the profession—the big dealers like Sidney Janis and Castelli—were ahead of the critics on this one.

42. A.F., "Pop Extremists," *Art News* 63, no. 5 (September 1964): 19. Another nice example can be found in Susan Sontag's review of Rublowsky's book on Pop in Susan Sontag, "Non-Writing and the Art Scene," in Gregory Battcock, ed., *The New Art* (New York: E. P. Dutton, 1966), 152–60.

43. Hess, "The Phony Crisis," in Battcock, *New Art*, 25.

44. Thomas B. Hess, "It Shouldn't Happen to a Hoving Happening," *Art News* 67, no. 2 (April 1968): 29.

45. I have argued elsewhere that avant-gardism derives its social authority by imagining two audiences—a real one of well-educated and like-minded connoisseurs (who are usually professionals or paraprofessionals) and a virtual audience of philistines who do not get it. Occasionally—as in the brouhaha about the National Endowment for the Arts in the late 1980s—this virtual audience becomes real. But more often than not it is imaginary, if only because this second audience meets avant-garde provo-

cations with indifference, if it meets them at all. See my "Desperate Seriousness and Avant-Garde (Mis)recognition in Some of Stein's Sentences," *Modern Philology* 97, no. 2 (1999): 220–33.

46. In this regard the story of Mark Rothko's aborted project to produce murals for the Four Seasons restaurant in New York is exemplary. In the words of James E. Breslin,

> Rothko had hoped to paint something that would ruin the appetite of every son of a bitch who ever ate in the room. Instead, the concrete reality of the restaurant . . . certainly ruined his project. . . . When he was working on the project, his imagination plus a dash of wishful thinking projected an idyllic setting where captivated diners, lost in reverie, communed with the murals. . . . It never entered his head that the works would be forced to compete with a noisy crowd of conspicuous consumers.
>
> Rothko, who spoke of his paintings in terms of unspecified "transcendental experiences," had always been ambivalent about the Four Seasons project. He expressed this ambivalence in his confused and confusing desire to create a sense of spiritual community with the rich sons of bitches in the restaurant and to ruin their appetites at the very same time.
>
> Rothko wanted the impossible. He hoped that a restaurant, a very fashionable one at that, could serve as a site of secular communion. But when Rothko actually ate there, the reality of the situation was devastating. It is hard to tell what offended him most: that his murals would serve as mere accents in the décor; that the restaurant itself was the scene of pampered appetite; or that he could not imagine the truly rich looking up from their expensive meals to contemplate his creations. In the end, he cancelled the project.
>
> *James E. Breslin,* Mark Rothko *(Chicago: University of Chicago Press, 1992), 405, 407*

47. Hopkins and Feld, *Philip Guston*, 41.

48. "Philip Guston Talking," in Nicholas Serota, ed., *Philip Guston: Paintings 1969–1980* (London: Whitechapel Art Gallery, 1982), 50.

49. For the convergence of different points of view of advanced art, see Buchloh, "Conceptual Art 1962–1969," 124.

50. Berkson, "New Gustons," 44.

51. Philip Guston, letter to Harold Rosenberg, March 4, 1977, Harold Rosenberg Papers, 1923–84, Research Library, accession no. 980048, Getty Research Institute, Los Angeles.

CHAPTER 2: THINKING THOUGHTLESSNESS

1. "When in 1968 Philip Guston abandoned the most restrained and elegant of all abstract expressionist painting styles for a mode of raucous figuration, I hated it. . . . Gradually, over more than a decade, I was brought around to the late Guston. . . . In itself, this story is only mildly embarrassing. Anyone who has a mind changes it now and then. But the tale seems worth telling, and for me is the token of an atonement, because my own experience coincided so closely with that of the art culture's reaction not just to Guston but to an epochal shift in sensibility of which he was a prophet and a pioneer" (Peter Schjeldahl, "Philip Guston," in *The Hydrogen Jukebox* [Berkeley: University of California Press, 1991], 227).

2. Lawrence Alloway, review of "New Paintings," *Nation*, November 30, 1970, 574.

3. Roberta Smith, "The New Gustons," *Art in America* 66 (January 1978): 100. Marjorie Welish fleshed out this argument a decade later. See Marjorie Welish, "I Confess," *Arts* 63, no. 3 (November 1988): 46–50.

4. Robert Hughes, "Art: Ku Klux Komix," *Time*, November 9, 1970; Harold Rosenberg, "Liberation from Detachment," *De-Definition of Art* (New York: Macmillan, 1972), 138.

5. Kenneth Baker, "Boston," *Art in America*, 62, no. 3 (May–June 1974): 114.

6. Debra Bricker Balken, ed., *Philip Guston's Poor Richard* (Chicago: University of Chicago Press, 2001). In his memoir of Guston, William Corbett refers to the book as *Alas, Poor Richard* and talks about drawings that do not appear in Balken's edition. I base my discussion on Balken's collection of drawings. See William Corbett, *Philip Guston's Late Work: A Memoir* (Cambridge, Mass.: Zoland, 1994), 50–55.

7. Philip Roth, *Our Gang* (New York: Random House, 1971), 190–91.

8. "Philip Guston Talking," in Nicholas Serota, ed., *Philip Guston: Paintings 1969–1980* (London: Whitechapel Art Gallery, 1982), 52.

9. I have not been able to find an instance of Guston's quoting Arendt, so my suggestion must remain somewhat speculative. It is hard to imagine that a reader as avid as Guston could have avoided the controversy around Arendt's book. In private correspondence Bill Berkson has told me that he remembers personal connections between Arendt and Guston in the mid-1960s (Bill Berkson, letter to author, January 22, 2004).

10. Richard J. Bernstein, "Did Hannah Arendt Change Her Mind? From Radical Evil to the Banality of Evil," in Larry May and Jerome Kohn, eds., *Hannah Arendt: Twenty Years Later* (Cambridge, Mass.: MIT Press, 1996), 141.

11. Hannah Arendt, *Eichmann in Jerusalem* (New York: Viking, 1964), 49.

12. Dagmar Barnouw, *Visible Spaces* (Baltimore: Johns Hopkins University Press, 1990), 238. See also Dana R. Villa, "The Banality of Philosophy: Arendt on Heidegger and Eichmann," in May and Kohn, *Hannah Arendt: Twenty Years Later*, 179–96.

13. "Philip Guston Talking," 52.

14. Ibid.

15. David Carrier, *The Aesthetics of Comics* (University Park: Penn State University Press, 2000), 73.

16. Ibid., 74.

17. "Painters Reply," *Artforum* 14, no. 1 (September 1975): 26.

18. Ibid., 35.

19. David Frankel, "The Rite Stuff: On *Art-Rite*," *Artforum* 41, no. 5 (January 2003): 8.

20. *Art-Rite* 9 (1975): 3.

21. Amy Newman, *Challenging Art: Artforum, 1962–1974* (New York: Soho, 2000), 383–425.

22. Max Kozloff, "Painting and Anti-Painting: A Family Quarrel," *Artforum* 14, no. 1 (September 1975): 37.

23. Jeremy Gilbert-Rolfe, in *Art-Rite* 9 (1975): 6.

24. Richard Hennessy, "What's All This about Photography?" *Art-*

forum 17, no. 9 (May 1979): 22–25 (see esp. 22–23); Barbara Rose, "American Painting: The Eighties," in *Autocritique* (New York: Weidenfeld and Nicholson, 1988), 273–89.

25. Dupuy Warrick Reed, "Julian Schnabel: The Truth of the Moment," *Arts* 54, no. 3 (November 1979): 91.

26. Ibid., 87.

27. Anita Feldman, "Space and Subjectivity: Four Painters," *Artforum* 18, no. 1 (September 1979): 49.

28. Hal Foster, "A Note to Painting," *Arts* 55, no. 9 (May 1981): 101.

29. The prevalence of this notion can be seen in Hal Foster's attack on it. See Hal Foster, "The Expressive Fallacy," *Art in America* 71 (January 1983): 80–83, 137.

30. Kenneth Baker, "Guston's Bleeding French Fries," *Boston Phoenix*, April 2, 1974, sec. 2, p. 13. See also Kay Larson, "From Abstraction to the Absurd: The Transformation of Philip Guston," *Boston Real Paper*, April 3, 1974, 20–21.

31. Thomas B. Hess, "The Abstractionist Who Came in from the Cold," *New York Magazine*, December 7, 1974, 102–3; Lawrence Campbell, "Philip Guston," *Art News* 74, no. 1 (1975): 90. Hess makes the case that the formal emphases of the abstract paintings caused viewers to ignore their anecdotal intent, just as the anecdotal quality of the new work made viewers ignore their formal interests. Campbell calls Guston "one of America's greatest painters" and sees the work, both early and late, as "a vessel abrim with stories, nostalgia and paint—and actually nothing has changed."

32. Noel Frackman, "Philip Guston at David McKee," *Arts* 49, no. 3 (November 1974): 19.

33. John Russell, "Guston's Last Tape Mislaid," *New York Times*, November 23, 1974, 38.

34. Ross Feld, "Philip Guston," *Arts* 50, no. 9 (May 1976): 9.

35. Peter Frank, *Art News* 75, no. 5 (May 1976): 134.

36. Bill Berkson, "The New Gustons," *Art News* 69, no. 6 (October 1970): 45.

37. Larson, "From Abstraction to the Absurd," 21.

38. Roberta Smith, "The New Gustons," *Art in America* 66, no. 1 (January 1978): 100. One can trace a similar move, at a higher level of abstraction, in Rosalind Krauss's "Notes on the Index: Seventies Art in America," *October* 3 and 4 (spring and fall 1977).

39. Hilton Kramer, "New Works by Philip Guston," *New York Times*, March 25, 1977, C18; Robert Pincus-Witten, "New York," *Artforum* 9, no. 4 (December 1970): 75.

40. Carrie Rickey, "What Becomes a Legend Most?" *Village Voice*, October 22, 1979, 90.

41. Carrie Rickey, "Gust, Gusto, Guston," *Artforum* 18, no. 5 (January 1980): 69.

42. "Philip Guston Talking," 54.

43. Samuel Beckett, *Three Novels* (New York: Grove, 1958), 414.

44. Here is a moment from the short story "The Expelled":

I set off. What a gait. Stiffness of lower limbs, as if nature had denied me knees, extraordinary splaying of feet to right and left of the line of march. The trunk, on the contrary, as if by the effect of a compensatory mechanism, was as flabby as an old ragbag, tossing wildly to the unpredictable jolts of the pelvis. . . . This carriage is due . . . to the period which extends, as far as the eye can see, from the first totterings, behind a chair, to the third form, in which I concluded my studies. I had then the deplorable habit, having pissed in my trousers, or shat there, which I did fairly regularly early in the morning, about ten or halfpast ten, of persisting in going on and finishing my day as if nothing had happened . . . and till bedtime I dragged on with burning and stinking between my little thighs, or sticking to my bottom, the result of my incontinence. Whence this wary way of walking . . . no doubt intended to put people off the scent, to make them think I was full of gaiety and high spirits, without a care in the world, and to lend plausibility to my explanations of my nether rigidity, which I ascribed to hereditary rheumatism.

> Samuel Beckett, *"The Expelled," in* The Complete Short Prose, 1929–1989 *(New York: Grove, 1995),*
> *50–51*

45. See the argument of H. Porter Abbott, *Beckett Writing Beckett: The Author in the Autograph* (Ithaca, N.Y.: Cornell University Press, 1996).

46. Carrier, *Aesthetics of Comics*, 96–103.

47. I am grateful to Archie Rand for pointing out the source of Guston's triptych.

48. Ross Feld, "Philip Guston's 'Wharf,'" *Arts* 52, no. 8 (April 1978): 147.

49. Robert Storr writes of this series of paintings: "One must look to Rembrandt to find a comparably moving or candid portrait of a marriage lived in the shadow of age and loss" (Robert Storr, *Philip Guston* [New York: Abbeville, 1986], 87).

50. Thomas B. Hess, "Dumb Is Beautiful," *New York Magazine*, March 29, 1976, 87.

CHAPTER 3: ALLEGORY

1. According to Guston, Piero della Francesca, like Albrecht Dürer, engages "all the world's essential forms" (Dore Ashton, *A Critical Study of Philip Guston* [Berkeley: University of California Press, 1990], 56).

2. "As to the paintings themselves and my own thoughts, there is a shift away from a scene being shown—towards more of an 'allegory', if I can call it that. Almost like a very plastic 'lesson' is being told OR GIVEN with tangible forms—Yet the 'plot' or 'story' keeps on to ricochet around. I am having a great time" (Philip Guston, letter to Harold Rosenberg, July 15, 1972, Harold Rosenberg Papers, 1923–84, Research Library, Accession no. 980048, Getty Research Institute, Los Angeles).

3. Ross Feld, "Guston in Time," *Arts* 63, no. 3 (November 1988): 41.

4. Robert Storr, *Philip Guston* (New York: Abbeville, 1988), 74–75.

5. See James Thrall Soby, *The Early Chirico* (New York: Dodd Mead, 1941), 13. This book was a favorite of Guston's, according to his daughter. See Musa Mayer, *Night Studio: A Memoir of Philip Guston* (New York: Da Capo, 1997), 58.

6. Feld, "Guston in Time," 41–55.

7. This is probably not as true of the postmodernist critics who seem to have relied on Paul de Man's "The Rhetoric of Temporality," in Hazard Adams and Leroy Searle, eds., *Critical Theory since 1965* (Tallahassee: Florida State University Press, 1986), 192–222.

8. Charles Rosen, "The Ruins of Walter Benjamin," in Gary Smith, ed., *On Walter Benjamin* (Cambridge, Mass.: MIT Press, 1988), 149.

9. Ibid.

10. Clark Coolidge and Philip Guston, *Baffling Means* (Stockbridge, Mass.: O-blek Editions, 1991), 36.

11. Ibid., 44.

12. Ibid., 84.

13. Most likely Guston would have found Panofsky's interpretation of the print in the English edition of Panofsky's work on Dürer, *Albrecht Dürer* (Princeton, N.J.: Princeton University Press, 1943). See Ashton, *A Critical Study of Philip Guston*, 54–56.

14. Erwin Panofsky, *The Life and Art of Albrecht Dürer* (Princeton, N.J.: Princeton University Press, 1955), 155–56. This is an expanded version of the 1943 edition.

15. Ibid., 168

16. Henry Hopkins and Ross Feld, *Philip Guston* (San Francisco: San Francisco Museum of Art, 1980), 40.

17. Philip Guston, "Faith, Hope and Impossibility," *Art News Annual* 31 (1966; pub. 1965): 101–3, 152–53.

18. Benjamin's theory of allegory is not central to this book of de Man's, though his groundbreaking "Rhetoric of Temporality" (1969) drew heavily, if not always explicitly, on Benjamin's work on the *Trauerspiel*.

19. Craig Owens, "Earthwords," in *Beyond Recognition: Representation, Power and Culture* (Berkeley: University of California Press, 1992), 41.

20. Owens, "The Allegorical Impulse," in *Beyond Recognition*, 55–57.

21. Ibid., 58.

22. "In its stead, Benjamin places the (graphic) sign, which represents the distance between an object and its significance, the progressive ero-

sion of meaning, the absence of transcendence from within" (Owens, "Allegorical Impulse," 65).

23. See Douglas Crimp, "Pictures," *October* 8 (1979): 75–88.

24. Lawson argues that painting presents the only option for the radical artist, because it is "painting itself, that last refuge of the mythology of individuality, which can be seized to deconstruct the illusions of the present." He lays hold of the critical disjunction between sign and signification that one finds in Crimp's and Owens's deconstructive rehabilitation of allegory to legitimize the practice of painting—a move that Crimp explicitly refused to make. Furthermore, Lawson locates painting's renewed claim to subversive vanguard efficacy precisely (and paradoxically) in the market's renewed interest in that medium (Thomas Lawson, "Last Exit: Painting" (1981), in Brian Wallis, ed., *Art after Modernism* [New York and Boston: New Museum of Contemporary Art and D. R. Godine, 1984], 61).

Kuspit defends German painting by claiming that the Germans do not fall back into a nostalgia for the naturalness of the figure. They recognize the disjunction between the material and the idea, medium, and meaning. They do not mistake cultural signs for natural wonders. Their use of figures is not a retreat to realism but rather an acknowledgment of realism's present impossibility. Because it is "déclassé," figuration is obviously playing with fictions. Because it lays no claim to representational truth, it deals with abstractions and codes, not things. See esp. Donald B. Kuspit, "Flak from the 'Radicals'" (1983), in Wallis, *Art after Modernism*, 143.

25. "The visual object/image has become the essential ideological correlate of private property" (Buchloh, "Allegorical Procedures: Appropriation and Montage in Contemporary Art," in Wallis, *Art after Modernism*, 48, 56).

26. This argument holds only for the Americans. Sandra Chia and Anselm Kiefer, to name just two, seem to wed allegory and melancholy—that is, to mourn the disjunction of sign and referent.

27. Lawrence Campbell, "Philip Guston," *Art News* 74, no. 1 (1975): 90.

CHAPTER 4: JEWISH JOKES

1. Musa Mayer, *Night Studio: A Memoir of Philip Guston* (New York: Da Capo, 1997), 237.

2. Dore Ashton, *A Critical Study of Philip Guston* (Berkeley: University of California Press, 1990), 190.

3. T. S. Eliot, "East Coker," in *Collected Poems and Plays of T. S. Eliot* (London: Faber and Faber, 1969), 180.

4. Mayer, *Night Studio*, 10–12, 19–20.

5. See Mayer, *Night Studio*, 22–14, and Ross Feld, *Guston in Time* (New York: Counterpoint, 2003), 91–92.

6. James E. B. Breslin, *Mark Rothko: A Biography* (Chicago: University of Chicago Press, 1993), 377.

7. Ibid., 57.

8. Dore Ashton, *About Rothko* (New York: Oxford University Press, 1993), 177.

9. Ibid.

10. Breslin, *Mark Rothko*, 377.

11. Ashton, *About Rothko*, 178.

12. That is not to say, of course, that one cannot trace Jewish content in Rothko's work. See, inter alia, Matthew Baigell, *Jewish-American Artists and the Holocaust* (New Brunswick, N.J.: Rutgers University Press, 1997), 100–109; and Matthew Baigell, *American Artists, Jewish Images* (Syracuse, N.Y.: Syracuse University Press, 2006), 63–75.

13. Here is Newman in 1948, before he adopted titles from Jewish texts:

> Man's natural desire in the arts to express his relation to the Absolute became [in a European art that followed the Greek ideal of beauty] identified and confused with the absolutisms of perfect creations—with the fetish of quality—so that the European artist has been continually involved in the moral struggle between the notions of beauty and the desire for sublimity. . . . The failure of European art to achieve the sublime is due to this blind desire to exist inside the reality of sensation . . . and to build an art within a framework of pure plasticity (the Greek ideal of beauty . . .).

In other words, modern art, caught without a sublime content . . . became enmeshed in a struggle over the nature of beauty: whether beauty was in nature or could be found without nature. . . . We are reasserting man's natural desire for the exalted, for a concern with our relationship to the absolute emotions.

> *Barnett Newman, "The Sublime Is Now," in* Selected Writings and Interviews, *ed. John P. O'Neill (Berkeley: University of California Press, 1990), 171–73*

14. Hubert Crehan, "Barnett Newman," *Art News* 58 (April 1959): 12.

15. Michael Leja, "Barnett Newman's Solo Tango," *Critical Inquiry* 21 (spring 1995): 561. In this regard see also Nancy Neild Buchwald, "Anxious Embodiments: Revenants of Post–World War II American Jewish Masculinities in Barnett Newman's 'Stations of the Cross,'" Ph.D. diss., University of Chicago, 2004.

16. Leja, "Barnett Newman's Solo Tango," 575, 577.

17. John Murray Cuddihy, *The Ordeal of Civility* (New York: Basic Books, 1974), 4.

18. Ibid., 13. "Intensity, fanaticism, inwardness—too much of anything, in fact—is unseemly and bids fair to destroy the fragile solidarity of the surface we call civility" (13–14). See also Cuddihy's *No Offense: Civil Religion and Protestant Taste* (New York: Seabury, 1978).

19. Newman sidesteps the issue by reading the Pauline thrust of Crehan's letter as a "twist of the Biblical metaphors of Mr. Nemerov's poem." The poem in question seems to have been Nemerov's "Certain Wits," although its applicability to the matter at hand is not as clear as it could be. See Newman, "Letter to the Editor, *ARTnews*," in *Selected Writings and Interviews*, 211, 216.

20. Margaret Olin, *The Nation without Art* (Lincoln: University of Nebraska Press, 2001), 169.

21. Thomas B. Hess, *Barnett Newman* (New York: Museum of Modern Art, 1971), 147. For another account of Newman's debt to the kabbalah, see Matthew Baigell, "Barnett Newman's Stripe Paintings and Kabbalah: A Jewish Take," *American Art* 8, no. 2 (spring 1994): 32–43.

22. Armin Zweite, *Barnett Newman* (Ostfildern-Ruit, Germany:

Hatje Cantz, 1999), 247. See also Baigell, "Barnett Newman's Stripe Paintings," 42.

23. Barnett Newman, "Response to the Reverend Thomas F. Matthews," in *Selected Writings and Interviews*, 287.

24. Hess, *Barnett Newman*, 60.

25. Barnett Newman, "'The True Revolution Is Anarchist!': Foreword to *Memoirs of a Revolutionist* by Peter Kropotkin," in *Selected Writings and Interviews*, 45.

26. By the same token, we can see a strongly Jewish, and not merely humanistic, self-assertion in the resolute verticality of Newman's works. As has often been noted, Rothko's paintings rely on fuzzy horizon lines and thus derive from a spiritualizing landscape tradition. Newman's canvases resist landscape and nature. Nothing could be less pantheistic than a Newman. There is no Spinoza there, no determinism, and no divinity leaking into your lines of sight.

27. Archie Rand, personal communication. In an odd way Guston might have been thinking about Soutine when he said this. In a discussion of Soutine that originally dates from 1951 but was reprinted in *Art and Culture*, Clement Greenberg attributes the painter's lassitude in the 1930s to his discovery that "bohemian individualism could not be literally and completely acted out in art." In other words, in the public and shared medium of painting, something of the bohemian's dream of a completely autonomous individuality would have to be sacrificed. Guston's reassertion of his Jewish particularity might have been an attempt to avoid such sacrifice. See Clement Greenberg, "Chaim Soutine," in *Collected Essays and Criticism*, ed. John O'Brian (Chicago: University of Chicago Press, 1993), 3:77–78.

28. Feld, *Guston in Time*, 92.

29. Ross Feld, "Philip Guston," *Arts* 50, no. 6 (May 1976): 9.

30. "Philip Guston Talking," in Nicholas Serota, ed., *Philip Guston: Paintings 1969–1980* (London: Whitechapel Art Gallery, 1982), 50.

31. T.J. Clark, *Farewell to an Idea* (New Haven, Conn.: Yale University Press, 1999), 382.

32. I paraphrase Cuddihy in this way so as to acknowledge Daniel

Boyarin's sense that Cuddihy accepts as true the anti-Semitic stereotypes that adhered to the *Ostjuden*. I am inclined to read Cuddihy's book (whose importance Boyarin is the first to recognize) as a form of ventriloquism, an attempt to recover the compulsions that drove the thinking of the objects of his study—Sigmund Freud, Karl Marx, and Claude Lévi-Strauss. See Boyarin, *Unheroic Conduct* (Berkeley: University of California Press, 1997), 39–42.

33. For a subtle discussion of this connection, see Freedman, *The Temple of Culture* (New York: Oxford University Press, 2002), 148–54.

34. The city features prominently in a painting Guston dedicated to Babel that I discussed in "'A Vast Precaution to Avoid Immobility': Philip Guston's *To I.B.* (1977)," *Burlington Magazine* 143, no. 1178 (2001): 296–98.

35. Isaac Babel, "After the Battle," in *The Collected Stories*, ed. Walter Morison (New York: Criterion, 1955), 187. I cite this edition because it is the one Guston would have used. Better, more accurate, and more complete translations have subsequently been published, including the sumptuous *Complete Works of Isaac Babel*, ed. Natalie Babel (New York: W. W. Norton, 2001).

36. "However it may have been, Argamak [a horse] had taught me Tikhomolov's style of riding [i.e., like the Cossack Tikhomolov]. Months passed and my dream came true. The Cossacks stopped watching me and my horse" (Babel, "Argamak," in *Collected Stories*, 200).

37. Babel, "The Rabbi's Son," in *Collected Stories*, 193.

38. Bill Berkson, "The New Gustons," *Art News* 69, no. 1 (October 1970), 44.

39. Mark Stevens, "A Talk with Philip Guston," *New Republic*, March 15, 1980, 26.

40. I am here relying in no small part on Benjamin Harshav, *The Meaning of Yiddish* (Stanford, Calif.: Stanford University Press, 1990), 89–118.

41. Roth's *My Life as a Man*—published after *Portnoy's Complaint*—is a brilliant and chilling reflection on the desire to pass in the literary world. For an account of *Portnoy* as a meditation on the ambiguities of assimi-

lation, see my "Harold's Complaint, or Assimilation in Full Bloom," in Sheila Spector, ed., *Romanticism and the Jews* (New York: St. Martin's–Palgrave, 2001).

42. "What I'm saying, Doctor, is that I don't seem to stick my dick up these girls, as much as I stick it up their backgrounds—as though through fucking I will discover America. *Conquer* America—maybe that's more like it" (Philip Roth, *Portnoy's Complaint* [New York: Random House, 1969], 234).

43. Roth, *Portnoy's Complaint*, 31.

44. Albert Goldman, *Ladies and Gentlemen—LENNY BRUCE!* (New York: Random House, 1974), 129–34.

45. On the kvetch as an art form, see Michael Wex, *Born to Kvetch* (New York: St. Martin's, 2005), 23–24. Actually, you should read the whole book.

46. Therefore an interesting aspect of the mainstreaming of what in the sixties still looked like "Jewish" humor is that the most influential *shpritzer* in America today is Robin Williams, a WASP from Michigan.

47. Perhaps it would be more accurate, judging from the reviews of the book at the time, to say that Roth is "too Jewish" a writer, an embarrassment precisely because of the vehement assertion of his difference.

48. Here is an example of the kind of Jewish joke I mean:

Two Jewish philosophers are deep in consultation. "Not to be born," says one, "would be the best thing for mortal men."

"Yes," says the other, "but that happens to scarcely one person in a hundred thousand."

The first philosopher quotes the pessimistic wisdom of Silenus, a fine topos from Greek thought. The second philosopher's clichéd objection is wonderfully obtuse, because, by definition, to be a person one has to be born. But this obtuseness turns back on the pessimism of the first philosopher. Not being born is not an option. So while the first philosopher might be right, his insight is certainly useless. I get the joke but not the analysis from Arthur Asa Berger, *The Genius of the Jewish Joke* (Northvale, N.J.: Jason Aronson, 1997), 159.

49. Morton Feldman, "Philip Guston: The Last Painter," in *Give My Regards to Eighth Street* (Cambridge, Mass.: Exact Change, 2000), 39.

50. Cuddihy, *Ordeal of Civility*, 232.

51. Clark, *Farewell to an Idea*, 382.

52. As recent scholars have noted, this absurdity haunted Greenberg's great early essays about art. In the mid-forties, Greenberg claimed that a "quality of Jewishness" was present "in almost every word" he wrote, and at the beginning of the 1950s he claimed that he, like almost every other Jew, was riven by self-hatred. In what ways, then, are his early theoretical articles "self-hating"? Lisa Bloom has read "Avant-Garde and Kitsch" in light of these comments and argues that, in Greenberg's view, "kitsch is tied to the constraints of ethnic particularism," and therefore all artists who aspire to greatness must forswear their particularisms, especially their ethnic ones. To become avant-garde, then, one had to cease being demonstrably Jewish. Similarly, in her account of "The New Laacoon," Margaret Olin shows that the formalist critic embraced abstraction because he, like many others, felt that abstraction was the royal road to a true universalism. But Jews had never achieved full abstraction. Expressionism, "the artistic practice of Jewish and other provincial artists," was "about the longing for unity rather than its achievement." To put this another way: for Greenberg as well as the Jewish Abstract Expressionists, the anxiety about achieving universality was always shadowed by the anxiety that it always lay out of reach, that they would be shown to be nothing more than the peddlers of provincialism and of kitsch. The parvenus, in their fear, would always be revealed as parvenus. For the Greenberg quotations, see Clement Greenberg, "Under Forty: A Symposium on American Literature and the Younger Generation of American Jews," in *Collected Essays and Criticism*, ed. John O'Brian (Chicago: University of Chicago Press, 1993), 1:177, and "Self-Hatred and Jewish Chauvinism," in *Collected Essays and Criticism*, 4:45. For Lisa Bloom's argument, see Lisa E Bloom, *Jewish Identities in American Feminist Art* (New York: Routledge, 2006), 26–27. For Olin's see *Nation without Art*, 176.

INDEX

Abstract Expressionism, 6–8, 12–
13, 21, 77, 89, 111n52; demands
on audience of, 25; modernism
and, 1, 24; painterly brushstroke
in, 17–18; Pop art and, 16, 22–
24; vulgarity of, 87–88
Agnew, Spiro, in Guston cartoon,
29, 31
allegory, 53–70, 103n2, 105n24,
n26; Benjamin's theory of,
56–57, 61–67, 104n18, n22; in
collaborations with Coolidge,
57–60; postmodernism and,
53–54, 63–65, 67–70, 104n7
Allegory (Guston), 54–55
Alloway, Lawrence, 19, 28
Andre, Carl, 6
Anglicanism, 73, 74
anti-Semitism, 32, 77, 78, 82,
109n32
archaic art, 58–59
Arendt, Hannah, 32–33, 100n9

Art in America, 63
Artforum, 19, 36, 38–40, 64, 65
Art News, 23
Art-Rite, 38–40
Arts, 23
Asher, Michael, 66
Ashton, Dore, 17, 46, 53, 71–72,
75–76
audience, 22–25, 62, 68, 97n45;
during Renaissance, 10; solicitation of, 2, 22, 70, 86; vanguard, 24
avant-garde, 2, 22–24, 64–66, 70,
81, 86

Babel, Isaac, 31–32, 80–84,
109n34; *The Red Cavalry*, 32,
82–83, 109n35, n36
Bad Habits (Guston), 43, Plate 5
Baker, Kenneth, 29, 40
banality, 2, 51–52, 70, 86, 89: of
evil, 32, 33, 35, 36, 48; of Soviet
realism, 81

Barnouw, Dagmar, 33
Baroque allegory, 56, 57
Beckett, Samuel, 41, 42, 46, 47, 86; *Endgame*, 41; "The Expelled," 102n44; *The Unnameable*, 46
Beckmann, Max, 1, 8
Bellow, Saul, 78
Benjamin, Walter, *Origin of German Tragic Drama (Trauerspiel)*, 56–57, 61–67, 104n18, n22
Berger, Arthur Asa, 110n48
Berkson, Bill, 100n9
Bible, 83, 107n19; Old Testament, 77, 78
Bloom, Lisa, 111n52
Blue Light (Guston), 48, 54
Book of Common Prayer, 72
Bourdieu, Pierre, 4, 5
Boyarin, Daniel, 108n32
Brauntuch, Troy, 65
Breslin, James E., 76, 98n46
Bruce, Lenny, 85
brushwork, 7, 42; painterly, 17–18
Buchloch, Benjamin, 18, 63–66, 105n25
Bunyan, John, *Pilgrim's Progress*, 55
Buren, Daniel, 66

Calley, William, 30
Campbell, Lawrence, 41, 68, 101n31
Capp, Al, *Li'l Abner*, 7
Carrier, David, 35–36, 47
Cézanne, Paul, 94n3
Cherries (Guston), 15–16
Chia, Sandra, 105n26
Chirico, Giorgio de, 1, 8, 66, 94n3; *Jewish Angel*, 55
City Limits (Guston), 7, 13, 14, 89, Plate 1

civility, 78, 107n18; alienating, 86
Clark, T. J., 87–88
Columbia University, 74
comic strips, 7, 21, 47–48, 54, 68
Conceptual art, 16, 25
Conspirators (Guston), 29
Coolidge, Clark, 15, 41, 57–60; "Signs Put Up on a Boundless Space" (with Guston), 58–59, Plate 8; "The Space Between Things" (with Guston), 59–60, Plate 9
Corbett, William, 99n6
Couple in Bed (Guston), 49, 69
Crehan, Hubert, 77–79, 107n19
Crimp, Douglas, 65, 66, 105n24
Crumb, R., 41, 42
Cubism, 8, 94n3
Cuddihy, John Murray, 78, 81, 87–89, 107n17, 108n32

Dangerfield, Rodney, 86
Danto, Arthur, 3–4, 93n3
Day's Work, A (Guston), 34, Plate 4
DeAk, Edit, 38
deconstruction, 63, 66, 105n24
de Kooning, Elaine, 17
Delacroix, Eugène, *Liberty Leading the People*, 55
Deluge II (Guston), 48, 54
de Man, Paul, 104n7, n18; *Allegories of Reading*, 63
Door, The (Guston), 50
Dürer, Albecht, 103n1, 104n13; *Melencolia I*, 53–55, 61–62; *St Jerome in His Study*, 61

Earthworks, site-specific, 6
East Coker—T.S.E. (Guston), 71–75, 89, Plate 10

Eichmann, Adolf, 32–33
Eliot, T. S., 71–75
Enlightenment, Jewish, 82
Ensor, James, 1
Entrance (Guston), 51
Ernst, Max, 8
evil, banality of, 32, 33, 35, 36, 48

"Faith, Hope and Impossibility"
   (Guston), 9, 12, 14
Feet on Rug (Guston), 50
Feld, Ross, 41, 49, 56, 74, 80, 96n32
Feldman, Anita, 39
Feldman, Morton, 19, 22, 86–87,
   89, 96n32
figuration, 1, 7, 8, 14, 73, 105n24;
   response of critics to, 22, 26, 40–
   41, 64, 99n1
Final Solution, 32
Fineman, Joel, 63
Fischl, Eric, 67, 68
Fisher, Bud, *Mutt and Jeff*, 7
Flatlands (Guston), 55–56
Foster, Hal, 40
Frackman, Noel, 41
Frank, Peter, 41
Freilicher, Jane, 6
French & Company Gallery (New
   York), 77

Gilbert-Rolfe, Jeremy, 38–39
Goldman, Albert, 85
Greenberg, Clement, 1, 8, 13, 26,
   37, 97n39, 111n52; *Art and Culture*, 108n27; emotions ascribed
   to kitsch by, 25; on tension in
   "painterly" abstraction, 14; vanguardism and, 22, 24, 81
Grey Gallery (New York), 39
Grooms, Red, 6

Guggenheim Museum (New
   York), Guston show at, 12

Head (Guston), 49
Head and Bottle (Guston), 43, 80,
   Plate 6
Head and Table (Guston), 80
Hegel, Georg Wilhelm Friedrich,
   77
Hennessy, Richard, 39
Herriman, George, *Krazy Kat*, 7,
   47–48
Hess, Thomas, 17, 34, 41, 51,
   101n31; critique of "vanguard
   audience" by, 23, 24; on New-
   man, 79, 80
Holman, Bill, *Smokey Stover*, 21, 54
Holocaust, 55
Hoods, 7, 28–29, 33–36, 43, 50, 52;
   of Marlborough show paintings,
   29, 31, 52, 55
Hughes, Robert, 19–22, 28
Hunter, Sam, 12, 13, 95n14, n15
hypermasculinity, 77–79

Jewish Museum (New York),
   Guston show at, 12, 14, 16, 88
Jews, 3, 70, 73–87; assimilation
   of, 78, 81, 84; nonobservant, 17;
   religous, *see* Judaism; Soviet, 31,
   80–84
Jones, Caroline, 22
Joyce, James, 86
Judaism, 3, 75–80, 82, 83

Katz, Alex, 6
Kiefer, Anselm, 105n26
Kierkegaard, Søren, 41
Kissinger, Henry, 31
Kozloff, Max, 38

Kramer, Hilton, 19–22, 24, 25, 40, 42, 89, 97n39
Krasner, Lee, 19
Kripke, Saul, 74
Kropotkin, Peter, 80
Ku Klux Klan, 20, 28, 29, 31, 83
Kunitz, Stanley, 75
Kuspit, Donald, 64–66, 105n24

Larson, Kay, 41
Lawson, Thomas, 63–66, 105n24
Leja, Michael, 77, 78
Levine, Sherrie, 65, 67
Lichtblau, Charlotte, 6, 19
Lichtenstein, Roy, 6, 7
literary paintings, 2, 15, 26
Long, Richard, 6
Longo, Robert, 65–67
Luini, Bernardino, 48
Lutheranism, seventeenth-century, 67

Magnet, The (Guston), 60–61
Malamud, Bernard, 78
Mangold, Robert, 6
Marden, Brice, 6
Marital Memory (Guston), 51
Marlborough Gallery (New York), 1970 Guston show at, 1, 7, 13, 15, 28, 41; Hoods of, 29, 31, 52, 55; postlinear representations in, 16; reviews of, 19–22, 40
Marxism, 63
Matisse, Henri, 34
Maupassant, Guy de, 84
Mayer, Musa, 18
McKim, Musa, 19, 49
Melville, Stephen, 63
metaphors, 3; Biblical, 83, 107n19
metaphysics, 57, 64, 73

Michelson, Annette, 97n39
Minimalism, 6, 16, 25
Mitchell, John, in Guston cartoon, 29
modernism, 2, 6–8, 11, 68, 70, 73, 87, 89; affective vestiges of mass culture proscribed by, 84; high, 19, 24, 37, 53; post-Baudelairean, 62; renegades from, 1; vanguardist, 23, 53, 81
Monument (Guston), 50
Monet, Claude, 94n3
Moon (Guston), 51
Morgenbesser, Sidney, 74–75
Motherwell, Robert, 75–76
Museum of Modern Art (New York), Newman show at, 79

Namuth, Hans, 37
Nation, 19
National Endowment for the Arts, 97n45
Nemerov, Howard, 107n19
neo-Expressionism, 40
"neo" movements, 69
Newhart, Bob, 85
Newman, Barnett, 3, 75–80, 87, 106n13, 107n19, 108n26
New Place (Guston), 11–13, 15, Plate 2
New York School, 7, 16, 24, 88
New York Times, 19, 41
Night (Guston), 49
Nixon, Richard, 29–31, 33–34

obduration, 60, 78
October, 63
O'Doherty, Brian, 18
O'Hara, Frank, 7–8, 84n3
O'Keeffe, Georgia, 6

Olin, Margaret, 79, 111n52
Outskirts (Guston), 35
Owens, Craig, 63–67, 105n22, n24

painterly approach, 12, 14, 16–17,
    25, 65; Pop's rejection of, 24
Painting, Smoking, Eating (Guston),
    44–45, Plate 7
Panofsky, Erwin, 61, 104n13
Paolo, Giovanni di, 94n3
Paul, St., 77–78, 107n19
Paw (Guston), 15
Paw II, The (Guston), 80
philistinism, 2, 23–25, 86, 89, 99n45
Picasso, Pablo, 1, 8
Piero della Francesca, 9, 14, 103n1;
    The Baptism of Christ, 9–10; *Flagel-
    lation*, 53
Pincus-Witten, Robert, 19, 21, 22,
    42, 52, 97n39
Pit (Guston), 54, 55
Pollock, Jackson, 37, 39
Poons, Larry, 6
Poor Richard (Guston), 29–31, 36,
    99n6, Plate 3
Pop, 6, 16–17, 22–25, 51, 52, 64
Postminimalism, 6
postmodernism, 2, 53–54, 63–65,
    67–70, 104n7
"post-Movement" art, 69

Ratcliff, Carter, 63
Rauschenberg, Robert, 65
Ravine (Guston), 51, 52
Red Eyes (Guston), 29
Red Sea (Guston), 48, 54
Reed, Dupuy Warrick, 39
Reinhardt, Ad, 8
Rembrandt van Rijn, 103n49
Renaissance, 10, 54, 86–87

Rickey, Carrie, 42
Romanticism, 56
Rose, Barbara, 39, 95n15
Rosen, Charles, 56, 61
Rosenberg, Harold, 1, 20, 23, 24,
    26, 28, 79, 97n39
Rosenquist, James, 6, 52
Roth, Philip, 30, 34, 84–86; *My
    Life as a Man*, 109n14; *Our Gang*,
    30; *Portnoy's Complaint*, 84–85,
    109n41, 110n42, n47; *When She
    Was Good*, 84
Rothko, Mark, 3, 75, 76, 80, 87,
    98n46, 106n12, 108n26
Russell, John, 41

Salle, David, 65–68
Samaras, Lucas, 6
Scared Stiff (Guston), 35, 36
Schapiro, Meyer, 17, 18
Schjeldahl, Peter, 28, 99n1
Schnabel, Julian, 39, 68
Schwabsky, Barry, 12
Sherman, Cindy, 65, 67
shpritzing, 85–86, 110n46
"Signs Put Up on a Boundless
    Space" (Guston and Coolidge),
    58–59, Plate 8
Silenus, 110n48
Simon, Joan, 63
Sleeping (Guston), 49, 69
Smith, Roberta, 28, 41
Smithson, Robert, 64, 5
Source (Guston), 48, 49
Soutine, Chaim, 108n27
Soviet Writers Union, 81, 83
"Space Between Things, The"
    (Guston and Coolidge), 59–60,
    Plate 9
Stieglitz, Alfred, 6

Storr, Robert, 54, 103n49
Street, The (Guston), 50–51
Surrealism, 8, 15, 94n3
Swell, The (Guston), 48

Tears (Guston), 49
Tiepolo, Giovanni Batista, 94n3
Tillim, Sidney, 37–38
Time, 19–21
Torah, 80
transcendence, 57, 64–65, 67, 69, 73, 87, 105n22
Turner, Joseph Mallord William, 94n3

Ucello, Paolo, *Battle of San Romano,* 53

universalism, 2, 48–49, 75, 79–80, 87–88, 111n52
unreadability, 35, 60, 61, 63, 80

vulgarity, 2; of Abstract Expressionism, 87–88; sentimental, 2–3, 69

Warhol, Andy, 17, 52, 62, 95n15; *Brillo Boxes,* 4
Wesselman, Tom, 52
Wharf (Guston), 48, 49, 54
Williams, Robin, 110n46
Wöllflin, Heinrich, 14
Wollheim, Richard, 10

Yiddish, 74, 75, 85

Text: 10/15 Janson

Display: Janson

Compositor: Integrated Composition Systems

Color: Pinnacle

Printer: Thomson-Shore